Schaumburg Township
District Library
schaumburglibrary.org
Renewals: (847) 923-3158

## Advance Praise for
# TRUTH BOMBS

"*This is typical Steve Deace: Well said, well researched, and not for those who like to be lied to. You can agree or disagree with his take on things. But either way, you'd be wise to at least consider what's in this book.*"

—Dan Bongino

"*Steve Deace is a man who has two very rare commodities in today's media: A nimble and curious mind and the courage to tell it like it is. If you are a Republican and vote the party line 'because we just have to win,' this book isn't for you, it is about you. In a clear and well researched voice, Steve gives you the truth of who we were, and who we have allowed ourselves to become. More importantly he explains why and how we must find our polar star once again, to lead the way out of the darkness of our postmodern world.*

"*P.S. This endorsement wasn't ghostwritten...you'll get the joke once you've read the book.*"

—*New York Times* bestselling author Glenn Beck

Also by
**STEVE DEACE**

*A Nefarious Plot*

WITHDRAWN

# TRUTH BOMBS

## CONFRONTING THE LIES CONSERVATIVES BELIEVE
## (TO OUR OWN DEMISE)

## STEVE DEACE

Post Hill
PRESS

A POST HILL PRESS BOOK

Truth Bombs:
Confronting the Lies Conservatives Believe (To Our Own Demise)
© 2019 by Steve Deace
All Rights Reserved

ISBN: 978-1-64293-022-1
ISBN (eBook): 978-1-64293-023-8

Cover design by Cody Corcoran

No part of this book may be reproduced, stored in a retrieval system, or transmitted by any means without the written permission of the author and publisher.

**Post Hill Press**
New York • Nashville
posthillpress.com

Published in the United States of America

This book is dedicated to the late Jonathan Narcisse, who nicknamed me his "brother from another mother." It's probably no coincidence, then, that my inspiration to write this book came right about the time he suddenly passed away. Because if ever anyone came to drop truth bombs, it was Jonathan. This book is my latest attempt to fulfill the calling Jonathan once placed in my life:

> *"When you're done on this earth, Steve, you want demons in Hell to wipe the sweat off their brow and say, 'Damn, I'm glad he's gone because he was a real pain in our sorry rear ends.'"*

Rest in Jesus, my friend. I know there are demons in Hell who have had it easier since God called you home.

# CONTENTS

# INTRODUCTION

This book was written to serve several purposes.

One of them is to educate you and show you truly where the bodies are buried. I've been on the front lines of this political/cultural war as an activist, consultant, broadcaster, and strategist for over a decade. I've had a front-row seat to the battle for the soul of America. And I would've been so much more successful if someone would've done for me what I am about to do for you. Treated me like an adult, and told me the realities of this war. As opposed to selling me on romantic notions of clearly defined sides, with ours being the one with the market cornered on altruistic motives. You are about to learn from my naive mistakes, and I pray you will grow in wisdom leading to more success than I've had as a result.

Another purpose of this book is to prepare you for that education, but to do that, I need to de-sensitize you, because much of what you've been told is either wrong or a scam, as this book will itemize and prove. To that end, this book will include several doses of tough love, with the intent of separating the wheat from the chaff. Consider this to be your political boot camp, if you will, where I am going to break you down to break your bad habits—in order to build you back up to be a total badass.

Along those lines, there will be times you may be tempted to tap out. To quit reading it because it's hard. But I would urge you to finish the race. Tough love is tough, but it is also love. If I didn't want you to be better than me, I wouldn't have taken the time to write this for you.

However, I can promise most of you reading this you are not prepared to do what must be done, because you haven't been shown what you're really up against and how the system truly works. Practical conviction matters as much in politics as moral or ideological conviction. If you are not prepared to do what it takes for your beliefs to win the day, it doesn't matter what you believe.

So never forget, fellow patriot, I'm doing this—provoking you to prepare you—because I love you and I love this country. And I want to see it conserved for our children and grandchildren.

So let boot camp begin.

Let's just set the proper tone right now and keep it real right from the jump—we kind of suck at this.

Oh, sure, we conservatives are selling more content and merchandise than ever before. So thanks for buying this book, by the way!

Nevertheless, the culture continues to cascade toward the leftist tipping point. Government continues to dangerously grow. Critical thinking on college campuses is increasingly imperiled. The courts are clearly out of control. The Constitution has effectively become a dead letter.

Dude, we don't even know what bathroom to use.

Unfortunately, our potential to combat these ominous political trends is limited, for there is no major political party in America that truly represents us. Instead of an existential clash, with a few exceptions, we have a progressive unibrow duopoly. With bickering denominations of progressivism (corporatist on the Right versus neo-Marxist on the Left) vying for control of the Church of State.

As a whole, the only real fundamental difference between Republicans and Democrats is this:

Democrats inspire their base to get what they want, while Republicans conspire against their base to get what they want.

Let's pause here for a moment, because the rest of this book isn't going to be worth your time if you're not willing to grasp what you just read. I absolutely loathe it when someone wastes my time, and since I'm commanded to love my neighbor as myself, I don't want to waste yours.

One of my favorite argumentation techniques is preemptively answering potential objections. I've got to assume at least one self-identified conservative objects to that bold text they just read regarding the real difference between Republicans and Democrats. If that's you, I'd humbly ask you consider a thought exercise.

As of the time this book was being written, here's a list of Republican senators in several of the most conservative states in the union, alongside their Liberty Score according to *Conservative Review* (which measures how faithfully they vote conservatively in Congress):[1]

| Lamar Alexander | Tennessee | 12% (F) |
| Thad Cochran | Mississippi | 24% (F) |
| Orrin Hatch | Utah | 27% (F) |
| John Hoeven | North Dakota | 28% (F) |
| Roger Wicker | Mississippi | 30% (F) |
| Johnny Isakson | Georgia | 31% (F) |
| Shelley Capito | West Virginia | 32% (F) |

| | | |
|---|---|---|
| Lindsey Graham | South Carolina | 33% (F) |
| John Cornyn | Texas | 35% (F) |
| Mitch McConnell | Kentucky | 38% (F) |
| Roy Blount | Missouri | 41% (F) |
| Bill Cassidy | Louisiana | 44% (F) |
| Bob Corker | Tennessee | 49% (F) |

A famous quote, often attributed to Ronald Reagan, describes the Republican Party's "big tent" philosophy this way: "The person who's my 80 percent friend isn't my 20 percent enemy." Well, how would you describe someone who isn't your friend a *clear majority* of the time? Most of us would definitely consider such a person an enemy.

And that's only looking at the Liberty Score of Republicans *who represent deep red states*, where presumably you're safe to pretend to be as conservative as you wanna be. The GOP has sunk so low it won't even lie to us anymore.

Points for honesty, I suppose.

Now, to complete this depressing thought exercise, compare the list of GOP betrayers to the roster of Democratic senators from swing states. Here is a sampling of their Liberty Scores at the time this book was being written:

| | | |
|---|---|---|
| Sherrod Brown | Ohio | 10% (F) |
| Michael Bennett | Colorado | 10% (F) |
| Tammy Baldwin | Wisconsin | 9% (F) |
| Gary Peters | Michigan | 8% (F) |
| Debbie Stabenow | Michigan | 8% (F) |
| Mark Warner | Virginia | 4% (F) |
| Bill Nelson | Florida | 2% (F) |
| Tim Kaine | Virginia | 2% (F) |
| Catherine Cortez Masto | Nevada | 0% (F) |

As you can see for yourself, Democrats in swing states— where both parties are competitive statewide—are collectively much further to the left than their Republican counterparts are to the right in their safe states.

And it's not even close!

Suppose American culture were a highway, with Republican leaders in one car and Democratic leaders in the other. While driving down that highway, they each come upon the same exit sign. It reads, "Next stop: ash heap of history."

Democrats would see that puppy and anxiously press the pedal to the medal, doing whatever it takes to arrive there as fast as they can—all the while calling everyone they passed racist/misogynistic/xenophobic/homophobic because they dared not be as orgasmic at the prospect of destroying the last bastion of liberty on this planet as they are.

On the other hand, the Republican Party would see that sign and perform the following steps (in order):

1. Check their mirrors.
2. Apply the appropriate turn signal.
3. Make sure their hands are firmly at ten and two on the wheel before conducting the necessary turn.
4. Double-check their seat belts are fastened.
5. Studiously obey all driving regulations and highway markers the rest of the way, especially the speed limit. They're the "law and order party" after all!
6. Make one last call to some corporatist donor, just to make sure that's still the exit they want.
7. Get off at the exact same exit and arrive at the exact same destination, albeit a little later than the Democrats who already got there.

8. Promptly gloat that while Democrats were reckless in reaching said ash heap, we should all be thankful they—the Republicans—were there to make sure we arrived at oblivion as safely as possible.

Elections don't seem to decide which direction the country heads in as much as the speed in which we go there.

So, no, I'm not throwing some click-baity hot take out there when I said there's little difference between the two sides of the unibrow. It's an observation based on the facts, which I just showed you.

Now it's up to you to decide what to do with those facts. I suppose you could close this book now, retreat to your safe space, and prove the snowflake culture isn't just for brainwashed millennials. Or, you could gird your loins and continue on. I'll wait.

Still here? Good. Let's take it again from the top.

We kind of suck at this.

And it's probably time to define the "we" here.

The "we" in this case are conservatives. Oh, and let me say this right now. Too many of you reading this are claiming to be conservatives, but you're really not. There's a simple way to tell if I'm talking about you.

If you're offended at what I just wrote, and thus contemplating tossing this book aside once more before it really gets started, then your butt-hurt reveals I'm probably talking about you. So go ahead, prove me right. Walk away right now and keep pretending that just because you're not a pinko commie, that somehow makes you the next William F. Buckley.

Because that seems to be what "conservative" means all too often nowadays. That you find Soviet-inspired political correctness repulsive and you aren't a communist. Talk about dumbing down your standard. We used to call applauding the freedoms of conscience and speech simply being an American.

So congratulations, you're actually paying attention, I suppose, and haven't given yourself over to the cult of progressivism (yeah, I said cult for a reason—more on that later if you last that long). But an America worth conserving ain't handing out any participatory trophies on my watch.

On the other hand, if my challenge to your conservative credentials didn't offend you, but like me you're tired of seeing the term dumbed down to it being meaningless, then you are the wind beneath my wings. Hop on board, for this journey is for you.

Maybe you're new to the political scene, and you want to know what conservatism really is and isn't. Or if you wonder why conservatism has not been tried and found wanting, but rather has been found difficult and rarely tried, this journey is for you, too.

Right about now, some smart aleck is reading this and thinking, "I don't even know who in the Sam Hill you are, dude, so where do you get off appointing yourself the judge of who or what is an authentic conservative?"

I'm glad you went there, because that's one of the key problems we have as conservatives. We have too many people defining what it means to be a conservative, rather than conservatism defining for us who are its people.

Somehow along the way, conservatism lost its way. It was permitted to be amended, morphed, or even outright bastardized to conform to the image of whatever fad or politician had taken hold of the Republican Party at the time. A mere prisoner of the moment, rather than a timeless movement. An instrument became an industry.

*See, conservatism isn't an ideology as much as it's an observational science.* Authentic conservatism comes from being an honest student of history. And then, from there, seeking to *conserve* for this and future generations that which has been revealed by history to be best for humans.

The root word of any word is what that word actually means. What's the root word of conservativism? You got it: "conserve." We are conservationists of that which has proven to be noble, just, beautiful, and true through time. We are so much more than a political party, or lack thereof.

We are stewards.

By assenting to be such stewards, we therefore give up our personal preferences, desires, and subjective opinions when they conflict with the objective truths revealed by history. For we are acknowledging there are forces at work in this world mightier than ourselves, and wisdom is first born by acknowledging God is God and we are not.

It is here we best emulate our founding fathers, who to varying degrees were fallen or flawed because they were just men. But despite their imperfections, they became *just* men (see what I did there?) by learning from history instead of believing they could arrogantly ignore or reshape it to their whims as today's postmodern progressives do.

That made them, wait for it...wait for it...wait for it...*humble.*

Ah, yes, humble, which means to display humility. You see that humility in how often they invoked providence (meaning the will of Almighty God), even going so far as to acknowledge that our rights come from God and not government. In the hopes that recognition would endow a government limited to how it can serve its people, instead of compelling a people to serve their government. That's the kind of humility that is in short supply these days.

Some of you might say, "Boy, Steve, you don't sound very humble. You sound pretty arrogant, actually."

No, I'm confident, not arrogant, and they are not the same. Arrogant is when you believe in *your* truth. Confident is when you believe in *the* truth.

The first thing any conservative must admit is *the* truth is out there, waiting to be discovered. But it will still be true even if we don't discover it, or choose to discard it even after we do.

A firm reliance on divine providence and history gives us confidence that we're headed somewhere as a species. That there is a cosmic plan. That there are good reasons for bad things, even if we don't know them yet. That all things will eventually work together for that greatest good, despite our temptations and toils as human beings. That one sweet day, we will look up and see our salvation is at hand. Good will ultimately prevail, despite our best attempts down through the ages to not make it so.

That's where my confidence in conservatism comes from.

I'm a kid born to a fifteen-year-old mom, who chose (thankfully) not to abort me in the early days after *Roe v. Wade*. I grew up in a home with drug and alcohol abuse, that all too often led to physical and emotional abuse.

I got kicked out of university because they apparently don't hand out degrees for majoring in *Tecmo Super Bowl* and party balls, especially when you didn't bother to attend a single class the entire semester. I wished they would've told me that ahead of time. I mean, how was I supposed to know you were actually expected to be a student—and on a coed floor no less? But I digress; we're all victims, of course.

Oh, and did I mention I met my wife in a hook-up chat room on the old, dial-up AOL, which might as well have been called "pagans in heat"? Heck, when we brought our first child home, her crib had to share a room in our crummy apartment with a porn collection that would make Ron Jeremy blush.

In short, I was conceived in, and then did, almost everything progressive utopians promise us is "freedom."

Except what I got from it wasn't freedom at all, but bondage—to debt, personal baggage and dysfunction.

To be a conservative is not to elevate yourself, but to come to the end of yourself. You seek to align your beliefs and behaviors with the tide of history, guided by history's ultimate judge, as often as possible.

What I'm really saying is *no one gets to define what or who conservatism is*, for what is worthy of conserving has already been defined for us.

That recognition also produces integrity—meaning a consistency (not perfection, because none of us is perfect) of belief and behavior. And if we fail, as we all will, to live up to the standard we claim, we have the humility to admit it, be held accountable, and try to do better next time.

If you want to know why we sadly have conservative heroes we used to look up to selling us out at every turn, it's because for them, for whatever reason, this has become about elevating themselves. Ego has replaced integrity. They are, ironically, like the very snowflakes they often mock for clickbait, arrogantly believing if it weren't for their presence or way of putting things, conservatism would melt away.

This is *always* where the sellout starts, and it's a pattern all too familiar in our pulpits as well.

If I should ever rise above my current better-than-average career prospects, I will be susceptible to it, too, for this is the human condition. Therefore by the grace of God go us all. So I won't mention any names here, because I don't have to. We both know some names already came to mind, don't we?

And when we as conservatives give up on that which is objectively true, and instead rely upon that which we subjectively scheme, we fail not just ourselves but our fellow man and families. We are no longer stewards but salesmen.

We devolve from patriots to partisans. And there are definitely differences between the two. Big differences.

Patriots preserve (or conserve) an exceptional country. Partisans allow exceptionalism to perish while they're busy posturing either for profit or position. Patriots believe in a higher cause. Partisans believe theirs is the cause. Patriots will defend their rights as citizens. Partisans will gladly trade their rights as citizens for political power. Patriots believe what matters is if the politicians support the people. Partisans believe what matters is if the people support their preferred politicians.

How can we tell if that's happened to us? Try taking this simple ten-question test:

1. Are you willing to even ask yourself "am I a patriot or a partisan"? Often a good sign we've yet to succumb is our willingness to self-critique.
2. Do you seek to politicize almost everything and almost every circumstance, or are you offended when others seek to?

3. Have you ever said the following: "I only watch/listen/ read [*fill in the blank of your favorite media echo chamber here*]. I don't trust any information unless it's from them?"

4. Do you alter your core convictions to justify voting for a candidate? No, I don't mean a willingness to choose between imperfect options. We live in a fallen world, after all, so we must confront less-than-ideal choices every day. What I mean specifically is, do you refuse to even acknowledge you're compelled to make an imperfect choice instead of deluding yourself by rationalizing the option you deem less painful is now heroic and ideal, when it's clearly not?

5. Do you really believe it every time a politician has said "this is the most important election of our lifetimes"?

6. Do you believe America's ultimate future is at stake in the next election, like you believed it was in the last one, and the one before that, and the one before that, and the one before that, and the one before that, and the one before that? Then, just days after the party you voted for won the election and took power, you found yourself already complaining about how they always sell you out? However, once the next election rolls around, you're back to repeating "the future is at stake" mantra all over again?

7. Have you ever compared a misbehaving politician favorably to King David, while ignoring the fact that King David's personal peccadilloes nearly led to the downfall of his kingdom—and both his people and his family paid heavy prices for them?

8. Do you define "fake news" as the news that isn't politically convenient for you to believe at the time?

9. Can you articulate what you're actually for better than you can condemn what you think you're against?
10. Is your excuse for constantly being betrayed by Republicans you helped elect that they're the "stupid party"?

If you answered yes to at least several of these questions, then consider this your intervention before it's too late and you end up cranky and miserable on the ash heap of history. If you answered no to most or all of these, then prepare yourself to remain on the narrow road. We need you to stay vigilant for the task at hand.

No matter which camp you're in, if you dare proceed with this book from here, you're about to get a crash course on how the truth can set us free. As in, free to see the world as it really is, not as we prefer it to be. Free from magical thinking, and on to critical thinking instead. Free from deception, including the way we deceive ourselves.

It won't be subtle, and it won't be gentle. But it will be necessary. I can't promise you this will be the best political book you've ever read, but I can assure you it will be among the most honest.

Bombs away!

# The Republican Party is Our Rightful Home

**TRUTH BOMB** *Political parties may be the single most corrupting influence ever devised by mortal man.*

The older I get, the smarter Thomas Jefferson becomes. While I prefer my theology with a more robust helping of orthodoxy than Jefferson fancied, when it comes to politics he was nothing short of a prophet. One of his keenest insights was on the corrupting nature of political parties.[1] Jefferson once quipped, "If I could not go to Heaven but only with a political party, I would rather not go there at all."

In other words, Hell—a place of everlasting torment, estrangement, and desolation that is the dominion of the devil himself (evil incarnate)—was preferable to perhaps our most brilliant Founding Father than spending eternity in paradise with political hacks. And while Jefferson was clearly being sarcastic, he may not have been all that far off.

At the very least, the myopia and internal corruption caused by undying allegiance to a political party is as much of a threat to liberty as any domestic dissension or would-be foreign invader. For it rots the soul, of both the individual and the nation at large, which results in the dulling of not just our senses but our intellect and integrity.

In other words, if we're not careful, slavish devotion to political parties makes us dumber and more deceitful.

A dumber and more deceitful populace is a lethal combo to liberty. It erodes cultural cohesion until a country is softened up to accept an unprecedented level of authoritarianism from the next false political messiah, who comes along promising "hope and change" or "I alone can solve your problems."

But a free people won't just leap from liberty to authoritarianism. They must be corrupted first by the status quo. In history, that status quo was often represented by monarchies, oligarchies, feudal lords, or empires. In our day and age, it is represented by political parties.

For sure, political parties can be, and have been, tools to do good. Just as not all monarchs, oligarchs, feudal lords, and empires throughout human history were evil. But once a people tie their identities and destinies to these earthly instruments, the clock is ticking on their sanity and character.

Once that happens, eventually will arise "a pharaoh who knows not Joseph" (if you get the biblical reference), who either wasn't a participant in the virtues of the past or wants to vanquish them altogether because raw power is preferable.

He will exploit the imbalance within the people—demonstrated by the fact they have lost themselves to the system—to acquire and/or consolidate power. Convincing them—via charisma, rhetoric, and exploiting their collective fear of the political alternative—their hopes ultimately reside with him. His demise means their doom.

This is how our two major political parties function nowadays. They each offer little in the hopes of affirmative change and far more often exploit the fear of the consequences of the other party winning. If only I had a penny for every time someone has said something like this to me: "I don't vote *for* anyone anymore, only *against* the other," I'd be as rich as Warren Buffet by now.

Democrats and Republicans offer you a lack of change agents on purpose, because at the leadership level they are creatures of the status quo. One party run by neo-Marxist progressives, the other by corporatist progressives. Collectively they are not proxies of an existential battle for the soul of a nation, but a unibrow.

This is why they battle most fiercely over procedure, like government shutdowns, and not principles, like what should the government's moral and constitutional purpose be in the first place? The former speaks to what empowers them and the system they serve. The latter speaks to what actually serves you.

They are not competitors in the traditional zero-sum sense, as in one side wins at the expense of the other. Rather, they are a duopoly. Since they're considered the only options that exist in the political marketplace, they both win regardless of what the voters decide on Election Day. All the outcome typically determines is how much *more* one party won than the other.

More seats on a committee. More positions of leadership. More office space. More negotiating leverage with lobbyists. More say in specific legislation. More reasons to genuflect to donors. More chances to virtue-signal for mainstream media acceptance.

But make no mistake, the "losing" party will have ample opportunity to do all those things just the same. Just as the size and scope of government is never really reduced (only if we're lucky they'll slow the rate of growth), so it goes with the so-called losing party after an election. They're not cut off from the levers of power—only given access to fewer of them.

This is particularly true after Republicans win elections, because they loathe their conservative base at least as much as the Democrats do. The Democrats may loathe us *philosophically*, but Republicans loathe us *personally*.

See, the people running the Republican Party seek to pillage and plunder the taxpayer every bit as much as the Democrats do, albeit for a different set of special interests and priorities. And they're just as eager to support America's slouch to Gomorrah as well. But they can't fully take the *Thelma & Louise* plunge[2] as long as they have to still pretend for our benefit. This puts Republicans in the untenable position of perpetually fighting a two-fight war.

On the one hand, there's the fight for power and positioning with Democrats, which on its own could simply be negotiated since they both want mostly the same thing anyway—more government, more spending, more amnesty, and so forth.

However, as long as Republicans must present the pretense of being an opposition party by paying us lip service, their negotiating power is diminished. Which brings us to the second front: the GOP's ongoing war on (not with) its own base.

This is why they rarely show resolve on our issues. They know they have to talk a talk they don't believe but will get killed by the liberal media despite no plans to follow through by walking it out anyway. So they get the worst of both worlds. They get killed by the liberal media for conservative rhetoric, all the while getting killed by their conservative base for having almost no record to show for it.

This creates a level of personal animosity for us even the Democrats don't have. You can see it in the way they come harder after those who would seek to challenge their power within the Republican Party than they do the Democrats.

Mitt Romney went hard after Donald Trump[3] as he was seeking the 2016 Republican presidential nomination (several of his criticisms of Trump I shared at the time). Romney left no flesh on the bone, going so far as to refer to Trump as a "con man." Meanwhile, during the final 2012 presidential debate, with a tight race on the line, the *Huffington Post* noted then-GOP presidential nominee Romney "agreed with Obama on everything."[4]

John McCain once ridiculed conservatives daring to challenge the status quo on Capitol Hill as "wacko birds,"[5] but when he was the Republican presidential nominee in 2008 McCain told conservatives "you don't have to be scared" of an Obama presidency.[6]

This came after it was revealed that Obama spent years as a disciple of a heretical, anti-American pastor, and described those who disagreed with a progressive remaking of America as "bitter" while they "cling to guns or religion."[7] As president, Obama would go on to preside over unprecedented intrusions upon liberty—like taking nuns all the way to the Supreme Court, demanding they disobey their vow of chastity to pay for the killing of children by the promiscuous.[8]

So, um, yeah, no reasons to be scared here.

There are so many more examples of Republicans fighting their own base harder than the Democrats, it would take an entire book by itself to catalog them. But I don't have to, because if you're a conservative reading this right now you're nodding your head in agreement, knowing this to be true. You've already lived it.

I've done my share of primary campaigns, in coverage and activism, all over the country. And if you don't think the GOP elites have a killer instinct it's because you haven't truly seen them try to kill. You're primarily focused on how they take on the Democrats. And you wonder why when the Democrats come at them with "you're a racist, misogynist, homophobic xenophobe bigot," most Republicans simply and blandly respond with something like, "I don't want to question the motives and character of my Democratic opponent; we simply disagree on the issues."

As a species, we attack most viciously that which truly threatens us. That's why the Republican Party typically attacks conservatives more viciously than it does the Democrats. With the Democrats they simply disagree regarding the pace and procedure for implementing progressivism. With us they *fundamentally* disagree on the role of government, what defines a culture, what the Constitution means. The list goes on.

Most Republicans are progressives, just of a different denomination than most Democrats, and one word defines the ultimate goal of progressivism in all its forms: *control*. Republican Party elites would rather lose elections to Democrats than lose control of the Republican Party to conservatives. This is why they fight us harder than they fight them.

To the Republican Party, we conservatives *are* the "them."

We conservatives see ourselves as the heroine Katniss Everdeen from *The Hunger Games*—reluctant culture warriors who really don't want to spend our lives in government but would rather live our lives away from "the Capitol" enjoying our families and the fruits of our labors. We only get involved because we have to, not because we want to. And we're out of there the first chance we get.

# LIE #1

We see the Left as President Snow, the authoritarian who uses a centralized government to maintain control of commerce and conscience—all the while his willing patsies/accomplices in pop culture (like Stanley Tucci's character Caesar Flickerman) dumb down the masses with empty calorie consumption on the boob tube.

Yet if you know how the story ends, you know there's a missing character here, a reveal that shocks the audience and shows the emptiness of putting your faith in political messiahs/parties.

At first, Katniss believes she's fighting for the freedom fighters of District 13, led by Alma Coin. On the surface Coin seems reserved, selfless, and not driven to extremes. Except it turns out she's been a false flag operation the entire time. Behind her technocratic exterior lies one just as cunning as President Snow, albeit for the interests of her District 13 instead of Snow's District 1.

Coin has simply been using the powerful symbolism of the courage of conviction driving Katniss, and those she inspires, for her own partisan political purposes. Once she successfully overthrows Snow, Coin continues on with the status quo. All that's changed is who has *control* of it.

Alma Coin is the Republican Party.

Repealing and replacing Obamacare sounded great, until the insurance cartel that fills Republican campaign coffers balked at actually having to operate in a free market rather than the guaranteed outcome government was giving them. Then Republicans suddenly didn't have the numbers to repeal it, after promising to do this for years and holding over fifty show votes. But dang if railing against Obamacare didn't help Republicans win over nine hundred elections nationwide.[9] Alma Coin would be proud.

7

On issue after issue, year after year, the Republicans similarly exploit our principles and policy ideas to get power, only to do almost nothing with them while in office as they maintain the status quo for their vested interests.

As a result, other than perhaps Second Amendment freedoms, virtually nowhere is America more conservative in terms of public policy today than it was *thirty years ago* when Ronald Reagan left office.

Right about now, some of you reading this are grimacing. Wanting me not to throw the baby out with the bathwater, because there are some good conservatives in elected office in the Republican Party fighting the good fight on our behalf.

I know several of those people. I even helped some of them get elected. And that's why I also know that if we gave them truth serum they would agree with everything I just told you. They're living it every day, frustrated beyond belief. I'm simply saying what they wished they could say and/or feel as if they can't.

The leadership of the Democratic Party is to the left of the average Democrat voter. The leadership of the Republican Party is to the left of the average Republican voter. So guess which direction we go regardless of who wins elections? The only debate is the rate of speed, and whose palm is getting greased on the way.

Today's Republicans, with limited exceptions, are yesterday's Democrats. They are arguing for the stuff now the Left wanted ten to twenty years ago. Want to know what the Republican Party will be advocating ten to twenty years from now, provided we allow it to live that long? Simply look at what Democrats are for now.

By the way, what was Katniss's solution to being used by Coin to trade one authoritarian regime for another? Why, she decided to spend the rest of her days going along with it, of course, because Coin was "the lesser of two evils" and she had to "vote against" Snow to save the country or something. After all, her favorite cable news host she loved more than her own children told her to.

Oh, no, *that's what we're doing with the Republican Party.* Neutering ourselves one election at a time, until all testicular fortitude is gone.

Instead, Katniss was all like "screw that noise" and put Coin down herself—proving that ballsy is, indeed, a fluid construct. Katniss figured she helped make the mess, so she had a responsibility to clean it up. She'd rather be damned then fight to settle for being the cog in a different authoritarian machine.

But Katniss wasn't much of a joiner. She was never indoctrinated into the system as much as she was estranged from it. So she had yet to lose herself to it. She never believed her identity or destiny was tied to sustaining the system. Rather, she thought sustaining the system threatened those things.

One instinct produces complacency, the other courage. Complacency turns us into partisans, while courage forges us into patriots. One is corruption, the other conviction.

Which of these are we?

Mothers and fathers will put up with betrayals and deceptions from their favorite politicians they'd never tolerate in their own children. All because they have what I like to call "the magic R."

Christians will turn Nebuchadnezzar[10]—the brutal, bloodthirsty dictator of the ancient world—into a positive metaphor for their favorite politician. Who once brought forth the children of a Jewish king, killed them all in front of him, and then plucked his eyes out so that would be the last thing the king would ever see. All because he had "the magic R."

Some of us will decide global gangsters like Vladimir Putin might not be so bad on second thought. The Ten Commandments might be mere suggestions. And when we once thought a president golfing every weekend was a sign of laziness, it's now such a tough job that he needs that break. All because he has "the magic R."

"The magic R" is more powerful than the hem of the Savior's garment. More powerful than the rosary. More powerful than the Apostle's Creed. More powerful than a seder remembrance. All who succumb to "the magic R" marvel at it and want to be like the one with it.

As their scriptures say:

"And it was bestowed upon him after the primary, the magic R, and he was credited righteous." *2 Self-Righteous 6:66*

The cynic might say this whole "magic R" thing sure sounds more like a scarlet letter, or even a mark of the beast, when you look closely at it. But, hey, the Democrats booed God at their convention once,[11] so that gives us permission to twist and turn God's Word as we see fit.

This is "God's Own Party" after all.

## LIE #2

# Donald Trump Corrupted Our Movement

**TRUTH BOMB** *Trump isn't our problem nor our solution.*

I think the best way for me to confront this lie some conservatives believe is for me to talk about my own history with Donald Trump. I was one of the first people to take Trump's presidential aspirations seriously, because I was one of the first people he seriously reached out to about running.

Trump sought me out because I live in the first-in-the-nation caucus state of Iowa, and there's been plenty of media coverage over the years of the prominent role that Iowa's status has allowed me to play in presidential politics. At least some (if not most) of that is overblown, but that kind of publicity isn't a bad thing in my line of work.

The truth is you typically don't have as much influence as your ego believes, but you probably have more than your detractors would prefer.

My record endorsing Iowa Caucus candidates reinforces that observation. Twice I have endorsed candidates early enough that I could spend months mining my network of contacts and maximizing my platform on their behalf. And both of those times, Mike Huckabee and Ted Cruz each set records for the most votes received by a Republican in the Iowa Caucuses.

However, I'm not so influential that I can simply make an announcement and the earth moves, either. I endorsed Newt Gingrich a mere week before the 2012 Iowa Caucuses, and he finished in fourth place.

Trump originally reached out to me through his former political consultant, Sam Nunberg, who spent years working in conservative grassroots politics for the likes of Jay Sekulow, among others. That experience gave Nunberg a leg up on who the real movers and shakers were when it came to building the kind of organization it takes to win in a place like Iowa.

The reason GOP big names so often flame out in Iowa isn't because crazy evangelicals like me, who put the fun in fundamentalism, so dominate the caucuses they become a tent revival meeting.

Sure, evangelicals do dominate the demographics in Iowa. But they also demographically dominate in the early primary state of South Carolina, too. Yet no Republican since George W. Bush in 2000 has won both a contested Iowa and South Carolina in the same primary cycle—despite those similar demographics.

See, in a primary state, name ID reigns supreme, which is why major endorsements can make a major difference. However, in a caucus state, organization rules the day. So when a big name like Wisconsin Governor Scott Walker comes to my state, as he did prior to 2016, and lines up the sort of key endorsements from the political class that moves the needle in a primary state, it barely registers here. Why? Because it's the activists, whom

Walker mostly neglected before bowing out before a single vote was cast, that move the boots on the ground.

And it takes months, sometimes years, to win over those activists—usually one handshake/photo op at a time.

That's why when Nunberg was laying the initial groundwork for Trump's presidential run, he reached out to people like me and my good friend Bob Vander Plaats, who is at the helm of the most prominent conservative grassroots organization in our state. He had Trump spending more time talking to people like us than our state's Republican governor.

Because, frankly, we were going to be more influential in the outcome here than the governor was, since we hang with the activists who actually decide who wins while our governor preferred the corporatists who fueled his ambitions.

Through Nunberg I got access to the direct line of Rhona Graff, who is Trump's longtime personal assistant. She would schedule Trump to appear on the syndicated talk radio show I had at the time, as well as make appearances speaking at grassroots political events in our state.

In January of 2014, the Salem Radio Network brought me out to New York City for a few days to audition for their new afternoon drive gig. On my first day out there, I contacted Rhona and asked if Trump was available to come on the show, figuring there was no way I'd get him on such short notice.

Sure enough, he made himself available. He was personable, informed, and scary good talking actual issues. At that time, he was being wooed by the New York State GOP to run for governor, so he was prepped for a serious conversation. He came across as someone you could see being a president, unlike the unpresidential persona many Americans currently know via his infamous Twitter tantrums.

I was right that it would impress the locals having him on, but not enough that Salem would eventually offer me the job (it went to former congressman Joe Walsh instead). Still, I was very thankful Trump made the time.

And it wouldn't be the first time he would do that for me. In fact, Trump endorsed my 2014 book *Rules for Patriots: How Conservatives Can Win Again* that this book is sort of a prequel to (more on that later). Trump told me to write the endorsement I'd want him to say, and if he liked it he'd sign off on it. So I did, sent it off to Rhona, and she got back to me with his personal approval of his endorsement I ghostwrote for him.

While I was auditioning in New York, Nunberg took me out to dinner at Ruth's Chris Steak House in Manhattan. We were there so long we shut the place down. As I look back on it now, it was during this dinner that it became obvious Trump really was serious about running for president this cycle (after briefly flirting with it in 2012).

As I was gorging on a plump rib eye, Nunberg asked me, "If you were setting up a campaign in Iowa, whom would you hire?"

I was suffering from meat sweats and not sure he was really serious, so I gave him a few names...all of whom the Trump campaign eventually contacted and/or hired a year later. And that's when I looked back on that dinner and knew this time Trump was really going for it.

It was the spring of 2015 and Matt Boyle, the chief political reporter/operative for *Breitbart News*, called to ask me about Trump hiring Chuck Laudner.[1] He was/is perhaps the best grassroots organizer in Iowa, and one of the names I gave Nunberg that night at Ruth's Chris. I knew Laudner wouldn't come cheap, because he'd be much in demand and had too much credibility to join a novelty campaign. So if he agreed to come aboard, it's because Trump convinced him he was in it to win it.

That's when I began telling all the national media people—who frequently hit me up for information on the Iowa Caucuses—to take Trump's aspirations seriously. Many of them refused to do so for months, even after Trump took over the national polling lead later on that summer.

In fairness to them, you didn't have to be a liberal media hack to have some healthy skepticism of Trump's chances, let alone his ambitions. Especially if you were at arguably the biggest pre-caucus political event that summer—the annual "Leadership Summit" hosted by the Family Leader, the influential conservative organization led by the aforementioned Vander Plaats.

Thirteen of the GOP presidential candidates were there, it was broadcast nationally by C-SPAN, and the event was moved to Ames to take the place of the world-famous Iowa Straw Poll (which the state Republican Party went out of its way to ruin before eventually cancelling it altogether for the 2016 cycle).

The establishment had just taken back control of the party from the Ron Paul revolutionaries. And it always detested the Iowa Straw Poll—despite it being a financial windfall for the party—because its emphasis on organization tended to favor (and elevate) candidates more popular with the grassroots. Otherwise known as the people who actually agree with what's in the party platform.

I co-emceed the event with Frank Luntz of Fox News and was scheduled to meet privately with Trump while he was there, presumably to close me on supporting and/or coming on board the campaign myself. On the surface it seemed like an odd pairing. After all, I am that dreaded Christian conservative your atheist college professor warned you about. And Trump is, well, Trump— noted heathen who spent most of his public life supporting the very liberal causes I've spent mine opposing.[2]

However, I'd just spent the last several years of my career fighting the establishment on land and on air in several primaries. And Trump did something very smart for being such a notorious big mouth: he *listened*. Trump spent more time reaching out to conservatives and our causes than Mitt Romney did prior to his 2012 run—more time than McCain ever did before or after he got the nomination in 2008. Furthermore, *Trump actually seemed to like us*, didn't treat us like redheaded stepchildren, and seemed to *want* our votes rather than *expect* them.

Of course, establishing this initial rapport is basic salesmanship 101, and Trump is nothing if not the consummate salesman. But that's what much of campaigning is anyway. Meanwhile, candidates the system preferred like Jeb Bush avoided us like the plague at best, virtue-signaled to the liberal media by actively opposing us at worst.

Trump did not try to sell us he was "severely conservative"[3] now that he was running for national office, as progressive Republicans like Romney had painfully tried to rebrand themselves in the past. He never claimed some "road to Damascus" moment on the road to Des Moines.

Instead, Trump chose to make the case that his previous, and documented, progressive activism wasn't what he really believed as much as it was simply the cost of doing business for a tycoon such as himself. Meaning he was basically paying off politicians (in this case Democrats when they're in power) for favorable treatment like lots of rich guys do. Trump told us he didn't believe in anything other than his desire to "make America great again." And if we could make the case that our crazy conservative stuff is what would do that, and help him win in the process, he'd definitely listen.

While many viewed succumbing to this pitch as a sellout, I never agreed with that. Not even when I was "Never Trump," and here's why: *it's the best and most sincere offer conservatives had received in decades.*

From the first Bush to Romney, every GOP presidential nominee for a quarter century had offered conservatives their own variation of the same Faustian bargain: decide which principles you're willing to betray to have a seat at the table. See the previous chapter for more details in case you've already forgotten the long train of abuses, and there will be more reminders to come.

Now, here comes Trump, who turns that paradigm upside down with this pitch: I have no principles, but I will adopt yours if you can sell me (and the voters) on them.

Let's face it: there was ample evidence in his life to suggest Trump was indeed malleable enough to live up to his end of the bargain. Throw in the fact the same elites who hate us also hated Trump, and you can see why the chance to etch-a-sketch a candidate for once instead of them etch-a-sketching us was enticing.

That's why I saw Trump as a blunt instrument: a human hand grenade, if you will, that I could toss into the toxic swamp to blow it up as a means of hitting the reset button. And I was angry at a Republican Party that had lied to me and others like me for so many years. When a man feels betrayed like that, he tends to listen more to his southern hemisphere (if you know what I mean).

So the prospect of making the system hurt, and then sitting back and watching the show regardless of the ultimate consequences, certainly appealed to me. Sure, that's more destructive than constructive, which is one of the reasons why the Apostle Paul urges us "in your anger do not sin." But when you've been betrayed as often as conservatives have, you start to relish the smell of napalm in the morning.

My anger was justified, but my willingness to lose myself to it was not.

Somehow during this time, I knew that to be true, and despite dancing with the devil in the pale moonlight. I never did ask Trump or anyone on his team what it might actually pay to climb aboard—probably because I knew myself well enough to know there was a dollar amount out there somewhere that might cause my conscience to take a permanent vacation, and the rationalizations to begin. I am a man, so I have an ego. Any man who claims he doesn't either isn't much of one or lying.

Character isn't found in not having a price, but rather the recognition of our fallen nature and not even tempting fate with it. That's why the Bible says to flee temptation rather than look longingly at it before attempting to white knuckle it while it's tantalizingly dangling there.

Boromir fails in *The Lord of the Rings* because he foolishly believes he is strong enough to resist the ring of power's evil, and thus only use its power for good. On the other hand, Aragorn is the hero by being honest enough with himself to admit he can't resist its evil, so he refuses to ever possess it.

At the same time, another candidate was tugging at my heartstrings—US senator Ted Cruz. I had dinner in Washington, DC, with some of Cruz's political team early in the primary cycle so they could pick my brain about the environment in Iowa. (I also had similar meetings with several different campaigns.)

I urged them to run because I always fear the longer anyone stays in Washington the more compromised they become. The swamp lives to put our champions in no-win Kobayashi Maru scenarios, in the hopes of proving to us it's impossible to stand up to the system by corrupting everyone. Therefore, with virtue unobtainable, we should all surrender now before it's too late. Resistance is futile.

From my vantage point, the clock is ticking on the depreciation of any politician once they arrive inside the Beltway. It's similar to how a brand-new car immediately begins depreciating in value as soon as you drive it off the lot. I call it "Ruling Class Virus" (or RCV for short), an airborne contagion inflicting the populace of the 202 area code for which there is no known cure other than term limits. Symptoms include a loss of integrity, forsaking of principle, and responding to your constituents' complaints against your selling out by claiming you're "governing."

Cruz had also invited me to Houston to lay out the vision for his candidacy, including a path to victory. That latter point was a major factor for me because we had previously sent two underfunded and understaffed conservatives on from Iowa in Mike Huckabee and Rick Santorum. Each had the superior message minus the resources to capitalize on it. All we did was delay the inevitable coronation of Mitt McCain.

This time, I was looking for a candidate who showed they had the message *and* the resources to go the distance. In Iowa we can give a candidate rocket fuel, but through Huckabee's and Santorum's eventual flameouts, we proved we couldn't build them the actual rocket. I was done with conservative protest candidacies and was now looking for a conservative who could potentially unite our base to defeat expected establishment front-runner Jeb Bush.

I knew Cruz well enough to know he'd be right on the issues, but other candidates would be right on the issues, too, in such a strong field. What I wanted to see was if he (or someone else) could build the campaign capable of *winning on or with our issues.*

That was something else that initially impressed me about Trump. From one of his first campaign appearances in Iowa at an event hosted by Congressman Steve King, Trump put a target right on Jeb's back, proving he was willing to do what it takes to win. Trump didn't care about second place, a cabinet post, or future standing in the party. To him, it was win or go home. He was from the Ricky Bobby school of competition: "second place is the first loser." He was speaking my love language.

Until I stood backstage at the Leadership Summit that sweltering July day.

I was waiting to meet with Trump after he finished his allotted time, and I had just heard him insult McCain not because he was a progressive Republican but over his valor on the battlefield as a POW at the Hanoi Hilton during the Vietnam War.[4]

That was followed by his admission that he'd never asked God for forgiveness because he'd never done anything wrong.[5] Throw in Trump saying self-esteem heretic Norman Vincent Peale was his spiritual guru,[6] and it was like the Holy Spirit had just done to me what Jimmy Cagney once did to Mae Clarke with a grapefruit.[7]

I stood there and looked around as if suddenly awakened from a long slumber. I remember looking at Ben Carson and his wife, Candy, sitting together and listening to Trump just bury himself with incredulous looks on their faces. "The media has been waiting for Trump to implode and this is it," I thought to myself. I even wrote a column along those lines for *The Washington Times*.[8]

Then I did something I'm not necessarily proud of: I bailed.

As Trump was walking toward me after his disastrous Luntz interview, we briefly made eye contact while he shook some hands. I thought he might ask me how he did, or how to fix what he'd just done. The only answer I had at the time would've been, "There is no fixing this, so get out now before you offend so many people you risk your kids and grandkids inheriting your empire."

So I bailed. I told those closest to me, "Trump is done." That night my wife said to me, "It's for the best. You know if we had gone with him he would've put us in indefensible situations like what just happened."

The next day we went to church and then to a movie. As we were leaving the theater, I received a voicemail from Nunberg asking me to call him right away. I figured this call would either be one last attempt to win me over, or letting me know the fallout was so great Trump was getting out now. Instead, when I called Nunberg back, he told me, "I'm sending you something right away and I want your reaction to it ASAP."

What Nunberg sent me was a column for *USA Today* titled "I Don't Need to Be Lectured" written by Trump.[9] In it, Trump gave a Milky Way Galaxy-size middle finger to those criticizing his crude comments about McCain, and even had the chutzpah to claim he'd done more for veterans than McCain had. Not only was there not an apology, but he had moved straight past doubling down to flat out owning it. If Trump wasn't going to ask God for forgiveness, neither would he seek it from mere mortals.

I called Nunberg back and told him, "Bold move, Cotton," and expressed my skepticism it would work. Nunberg shot back, "You should recognize this strategy, Steve, it's right out of your book."[10]

I politely ended the call, thinking this might be the last time Nunberg and I ever talk as Trump returns to lifestyles of the rich and famous while the rest of us not wealthy enough to be immune to a cultural collapse attempt to save whatever is left of Western Civilization.

Boy, was I wrong.

Not only have Nunberg and I remained friendly these past few years, but a week or so after I thought Trump's campaign was toast I called Laudner. By this point I had moved on to narrowing my list to Cruz, Huckabee, Walker, and Louisiana governor Bobby Jindal—candidates who had proven to be much closer to my beliefs than Trump. I was thinking that when it came to my Trump flirtation, I had dodged a bullet. Garth Brooks was right again: thank God for unanswered prayers.

I expected Laudner to tell me the USS *Trump* was taking on water, and maybe we'd even discuss who his plan B was, but that's not what he told me. Instead, Laudner said that although he was also offended by Trump's comments and prepared to walk at first, he was blown away by the response Trump was getting.

"I've never gotten so much positive reaction to anything during my time in politics," he told me. "So many people, even veterans who think Trump's comments were appalling, have contacted our campaign to thank us for not backing down afterward. People are so sick and tired of spineless politicians, and they hate the media, so they're excited to see someone stick to their guns even if they didn't agree with what he said."

In August my wife and I decided to publicly support Cruz, and I went to work for the campaign a few months later. I still didn't think Trump was going to win Iowa or the nomination, but I thought he might help us do it. Trump could clear a path by toppling Jeb for us while we worked to coalesce conservatives off on our own. Which we eventually did in December, when an unprecedented coalition of conservative groups/leaders, who typically splintered during GOP presidential primaries, coalesced behind Cruz.

I didn't become "Never Trump" by supporting Cruz. Quite the contrary, I originally encouraged us to have good relations with Trump and his campaign because both of us appealed to the antiestablishment fervor sweeping the grassroots. The dumbest strategy either of us could've pursued was to confront each other before it was the right time. That would be mutually assured destruction, which is why GOP establishment-friendly media was demanding it.

I even encouraged Cruz to avoid Trump, yea or nay, when I was on his prep team for the GOP Colorado debate that October. I wanted him to focus on making the case that he was the conservative who could coalesce our base and win, while everyone else was ganging up on front-runner Trump.

The reason Marco Rubio's campaign/allies and others complained publicly about the Cruz-Trump détente (to the best of my knowledge there was never an official alliance as they claimed) was because it hindered their chances to be successful. But it wasn't our job to concoct a favorable strategy for them—only for us.

So how did I evolve from almost getting in on the ground floor of the Trump campaign to "Never Trump" in less than eight months?

November 13, 2015 was a galvanizing moment for me.

That was the date of Trump's unhinged tirade directed at Carson, who had just surpassed him in the national polls.[11] While I had already determined Carson wasn't ready for prime time politically, Trump set out to personally destroy one of America's last living legends in what can only be described as a meltdown unbecoming of a basic adult, let alone the most powerful man in the world. He even went so far as to call Iowans "stupid" for believing in Carson's quintessential American success story.

This was no mere political attack. I'm no shrinking violet, mind you, and when it comes to issues, I encourage the candidates I work for and/or support to shoot to kill (metaphorically speaking). This was petty, vindictive, and unstable. Carson's sin wasn't his inconsistent pro-life position that *Politico* called "perplexing" during the primary.[12] Nor was it anything in his private life that would disqualify him from the presidency.

In Trump's mind, Carson was worthy of being disemboweled because he stood in the way of something Trump wanted and nothing more. At least when Trump attacked Jeb he did so based mostly on whether he was capable of winning. But this thing with Carson was different. It was, for lack of a better word, disturbing.

It was another clarifying moment for me where Trump was concerned, especially because we've seen so many sad scenes just like it since then. This was not some isolated incident in the heat of an exhausting campaign. These are people, not robots, and sometimes people, even good ones, show their arse. Lord knows I've done it a time or two. We're only human.

But Trump treated Carson like he was subhuman for no sin other than polling higher than he was at the time. Yes, I like to win, but not at the expense of my own soul. I simply couldn't abide his treating a Christian brother like Carson in such a way. As we would later learn, this wasn't Trump simply losing his cool one time. This was the dawn of a new, unfortunate phase of his campaign. He was about to become the 2 Live Crew of politics— as nasty as he wanna be.

From there, we would go on to see an unprecedented list of people clown and corrupt themselves in order to serve Trump. Craven opportunists lined up as if they were legion to ride Trump's coattails to prominence. Many of them were heretofore unheard of or tarnished beyond repair (we're looking at you, Chris Christie)[13], before crawling out from underneath whatever rot-infested rock they were previously inhabiting prior to answering Trump's siren song.

It got so incestuous that Trump's minions even hilariously slimed his own campaign spokeswoman, Katrina Pierson,[14] while they were trying to smear Cruz, whom they claimed was unlikable and robotic, yet somehow was also the Mac Daddy of the US Senate. Got it.

I once confronted one of them on national television, asking her, "Do you have any integrity at all?" in response to her clear dishonesty.[15] Not the political obfuscation we've become accustomed to—this was clear dishonesty. She would go on to become the national spokeswoman for the Republican Party.

Let that simmer for a second.

Hers is a story that has been repeated often since Trump first came down the escalator to formally announce his candidacy. Perhaps no politician in American history has simultaneously exposed, ended, and rewarded as many frauds as Trump has.

Trump is many things—some good and some bad—but politically he is a clarifier above all.

If you come into Trump's orbit, the force of his personality and its demands will clarify your motivations, desires, and character. He has revealed just how corrupt our system of government is by the extent it's willing to go to either subdue or serve him.

This is why I was "Never Trump," which ended for me after he won the election. Now it's about what's best for the country as far as I'm concerned, not attempting to justify my previous position on him one way or another. Besides, if I think I'm right and can defend why, I frankly don't give a rip what anyone thinks anyway.

I wasn't "Never Trump" for any reason other than I didn't think he would govern conservative enough to justify gambling on his obvious character concerns. But now that the people have had their say, I will respect their will. Nor will I actively root against an American president. I will, however, oppose him when I think he's wrong.

Thankfully, Trump has actually performed better as president from a policy perspective than I anticipated. He was actually on quite a roll at the time I was writing this book, checking several domestic and foreign policy boxes conservatives care about. This prompted me to poll my audience, not always the most pro-Trump crowd on the Right, to find out if they thought Trump had accomplished more in his first sixteen months on the job than either a President Romney or McCain would have.[16]

A whopping 78 percent of my audience said yes, and when I asked them why, these were some of their comments:

- ▶ "Romney and McCain would've been very liberal progressive presidents, so they would've worked with the unibrow party to pass more government programs and thus more government control."

- ▶ "It depends on whether you count all the wars McCain would've likely started as president as progress."
- ▶ "Best case scenario is McCain wouldn't have made it worse."
- ▶ "No way does Romney or McCain leave sham Paris accords or move the embassy, let alone take on the EPA."

In other words, they had lost hope that those more dignified, nice-guy Republicans would have delivered for them after years of evidence to the contrary. Because whenever those candidates do win, once in office they become Swamp Things and do the bidding of K Street and the liberal media instead of the everyday conservatives who voted to put them there.

They have grown tired of being the forty-year-old bride-to-be who shows up at the bridal shop and requests a gown with a veil only to have the attendant politely explain to her such gowns are traditionally reserved for more virginal brides.

"I'll have you know I'm as virginal as the women half my age pretend to be prior to their weddings even though this will be my fourth marriage," the would-be bride says, offended at the arrogance of the attendant.

"Pardon me, madam, but how is that possible given your age?" the shop attendant presses.

"Well, I got into a terrible argument with my first husband on the way to the reception, so we realized this was a mistake and had the marriage annulled," the woman explains. "Then, my second husband got so excited just as we were about to consummate the marriage, he tragically suffered a heart attack and died."

"That's so sad," the attendant replies, "but what about your third husband?"

The woman then drops the punch line: "Well, he was an establishment Republican, you see, so he just sat on the edge of the bed and told me how good it was going to be for years."

I wish I could tell you this joke was my own, but it's not. Ronald Reagan used to tell this one back in the day. However, he told it about Democrats. I inserted "establishment Republican" instead, because the GOP has become so treacherous the joke deserved to be updated.

Except the joke has actually been on us—at our expense.

So Trump may be the Wizard of Oz. He may be more con man than great and terrible, and his Twitter account may be the political equivalent of the man behind the curtain pretending to be a powerful sorcerer when he's really not. But he still helps Dorothy return home at the end of the movie, doesn't he? The journey still ends with the defeat of the Wicked Witch of the West, doesn't it? And in a kingdom where Dorothy's allies lack courage, heart, and smarts—three necessary traits systemically lacking in today's GOP as well—even a pretend wizard is better than no wizard at all.

Sure, the obvious character flaws are still there, and they flare up consistently. But his aren't the only character flaws that show themselves. Nor are they relegated to his court of owls, otherwise known as his shills and apologists.

To be clear, I'm not including good people attempting to serve the country by serving in his White House in that "court of owls" reference. How can you tell the difference? The good people are the ones who can make Trump sound/appear more presidential, stable, and adult. The court of owls are the ones who wouldn't be there unless Trump were frequently unpresidential, unstable, and childish.

Since the election we've also seen some of my previous "Never Trump" brethren clowning themselves as well. Turns out they didn't oppose Trump for ideological or even moral reasons, like me or a few others on the Right did. Their opposition to Trump stemmed from losing control of the Republican Party to his base of everyday Americans, which they find just as deplorable as the Left does.

And now they're infesting our news channels by deciding what they're for or against on the basis of what Trump says or does—just like his worm tongues they used to mock. It turns out "Never Trump" can be just as corrupting as "Always Trump."

Much of what's called "Trump analysis" these days falls into one of these two camps: people who would have no career if not for their shameless willingness to proclaim Trump as fearless leader no matter what, or people who blame absolutely anything and everything on Trump. Usually, if you're not willing to twist your soul into one of these cults, your opinion isn't sought out.

As a producer at a major news network told me once, "We're looking for *sides* more than just *opinions.*"

These two jokes aren't in opposition as much as they're two sides of the same coin. One side conforms to Trump, the other away from. Each treat him as if he's a god. They each have an unhealthier obsession with Trump than he does with himself, and when you consider Trump's full-blown narcissism, that is hard to do.

To each, Trump is the precious, the object of an extreme and unhealthy love-hate relationship that twists and distorts who they once were—turning them into Gollums. They would be nothing politically without Trump, their positions defined by either licking his boots or kicking him in the shins.

As for me, I'm fine agreeing with Trump when he does something I support, and disagreeing with him when he does not. Sure, it doesn't land me as many TV hits or lucrative speaking engagements as I otherwise would by joining one of these islands of misfit toys, but I'm kind of a loner anyways.

I started off thinking Trump might be the solution, until I was reminded of his deep character flaws. I then went to the opposite extreme with "Never Trump," and now I've witnessed a very flawed man doing some very good things.

Both of these positions of mine were reactionary and not rooted in truth as much as my reaction to what the truth actually was. That truth is this: Trump is neither the cause nor solution to our problems as conservatives.

Trump is just a charismatic but fallen figure who represents the culture from whence he came. Really a bit player in the long run. No one took him seriously politically five years ago, and five minutes after he's gone no one will, either. For eight years it was like Barack Obama was omnipresent. Now he's barely an afterthought.

If we had a healthier movement, or any kind of a movement at all, we could mold such an amorphous organism as Trump to our bidding far more often than we do. Heck, we've already gotten some things out of Trump we've been unable to get conventional/family guy Republicans to try or do, as problematic as he is.

But we're too busy debating whether he's Cheeto Jesus or the Anti-Christ. Why? Because defending Trump when he's indefensible, or attacking him ruthlessly when he's right, is good for business. And we've gots to get dem clicks, yo. We're more like Suge Knight than Walter Cronkite. More Death Row Records than *Firing Line.*

Too much of our audience apparently demands Trump to either be perpetually vile or victim and has little appetite for simply demanding he be a good president. So they're spoon-fed what I call "infotainment," with media platforms feeding content to a target audience that feeds the narrative that audience prefers.

So if Trump didn't corrupt our movement but just capitalized on the corruption that was already there, what did? That will be answered in upcoming chapters.

# Republicans are the Pro-Life Party

**TRUTH BOMB** *A political party that will not even defund its own sworn enemy doesn't deserve to live.*

To truly grasp the full breadth of the Republican Party's betrayal of its pro-life base, a history lesson is required.

Let's go back to an America before the child killing industry had truly gone mainstream: the dawn of the *Roe v. Wade* era. Before Planned Parenthood had taken over the Democratic Party. Back when people were writing things like this:

The question of abortion confronts me in several different ways. First, although I do not profess to be a biologist, I have studied biology and know something about life from the point of view of the natural sciences. Second, I am a minister of the Gospel and therefore, feel that abortion has a religious and moral dimension that I must consider. Third, I was born out of wedlock (and against the advice that my mother received from her doctor) and therefore abortion is a personal issue for me. From my perspective, *human life is the highest good, and God is the supreme good because He is the giver of life.* That is my philosophy. Everything I do proceeds from that religious and philosophical premise.

Therefore, life is the highest human good *because life is sacred.* Biologically speaking, thousands of male sperms are ejaculated into the female reproductive tract during sexual intercourse, but only once in a while do the egg and sperm bring about fertilization. Some call that connection accidental, but I choose to call it providential. *It takes three to make a baby: a man, a woman, and the Holy Spirit.*

Human beings cannot give or create life by themselves; it is really a gift from God. Therefore, one does not have the right to take away (through abortion) that which he does not have the ability to give.

Some of the most dangerous arguments for abortion stem from popular judgments about life's ultimate meaning, but the logical conclusion of their position is never pursued. Some people may, unconsciously, operate their lives as if pleasure is life's highest good, and pain and suffering man's greatest enemy. That position, if followed to its logical conclusion, means that which prohibits pleasure should be done away with by whatever means are necessary.

By the same rationale, whatever means are necessary should be used to prevent suffering and pain. My position is not to negate pleasure nor elevate suffering, but merely to argue against their being elevated to an ultimate end of life. Because if they are so elevated, anything, including murder and genocide, can be carried out in their name.

Psychiatrists, social workers, and doctors often argue for abortion on the basis that the child will grow up mentally and emotionally scarred. But who of us is complete? If incompleteness were the criteria for taking life we would all be dead. If you can justify abortion on the basis of emotional incompleteness, then your logic could also lead you to killing for other forms of incompleteness—blindness, crippleness, and old age.

There are those who argue that the right to privacy is of higher order than the right to life. I do not share that view. I believe that life is not private, but rather it is public and universal. If one accepts the position that life is private, and therefore you have the right to do with it as you please, one must also accept the conclusion of that logic. *That was the premise of slavery.* You could not protest the existence or treatment of slaves on the plantation because that was private and therefore outside of your right to be concerned.

Another area that concerns me greatly, *namely because I know how it has been used with regard to race*, is the psycholinguistics involved in this whole issue of abortion. If something can be dehumanized through the rhetoric used to describe it, then the major battle has been won. *That is why the Constitution called us three-fifths human and then whites further dehumanized us by calling us "n*****s." It was part of the dehumanizing process. The first step was to distort the image of us as human beings in order to justify that which they wanted to do and not even feel like they had done anything wrong. Those advocates of taking life prior to birth do not call it killing or murder; they call it abortion. They further never talk about aborting a baby because that would imply something human. Rather they talk about aborting the fetus. Fetus sounds less than human and therefore can be justified.*

It is that question, the question of our attitude, our value system, and our mind-set with regard to the nature and worth of life itself, *that is the central question confronting mankind. Failure to answer that question affirmatively may leave us with a hell right here on earth.*[1] [emphasis added throughout]

What you just read is perhaps the finest pro-life apologetic I have ever encountered, and I have read and written/given more than my share. I've probably spoken more on life than any other issue in my career.

Would you like to know who wrote it?

What if I were to tell you those were once the words of Jesse Jackson? Yep, *that* Jesse Jackson. Hero of the pro-child-killing Left, who nowadays flees when confronted with the black genocide caused by abortion.[2]

But forty years ago, Jackson was saying things about the life issue we can't get 99 percent of the Republicans from the alleged "pro-life party" to say today—let alone act upon. To make matters worse, what if I were to tell you that if not for *Roe v. Wade*, Republicans might not have won a single national election post-Watergate? At the very least, there never would've been a Reagan Revolution without *Roe v. Wade*.

Think all that's far-fetched or an overreach? Think again. Let's go back to our history lesson, shall we?

*Roe v. Wade*, the original Supreme Court *opinion* (courts don't make law, which I will elaborate on later) that gave birth to the infanticide holocaust, came down in January of 1973. It was right after a fourteen-year-old girl had learned over Christmas break she was pregnant by her high school sweetheart. Suddenly she had a decision to make. Several of her friends had gotten illegal abortions, but now she had the option of killing her child "safe" and "legal."

In the end, after wrestling with her conscience, she couldn't bring herself to do it, and seven months later the now fifteen-year-old Vickie gave birth to her son at Iowa Lutheran Hospital on July 28, 1973.

I am her son.

Therefore, as you can see, the issue of life is not only a moral, philosophical, and theological one for me (besides, I couldn't make those arguments any better than what I've already quoted from Jesse Jackson anyway). It's also *personal*. I am here despite what the government would've permitted my mother to do to me, and thus so are my children and eventually their children and so on and so forth.

We often neglect the personal cost of erasing a generation of our children before they were born. Statistics are so horrifying and staggering they seem clinical and inaccessible. So let's bring the point home by making it personal for a moment.

Who's to say one of those children wouldn't have cured cancer or another deadly disease? Invented some revolutionary form of renewable, clean energy? Or a technology that allowed impoverished nations to join the modern age? Maybe they might've just been the loving spouse you or someone you care about still hasn't been able to find?

The political landscape at this time was much different than the one we have today. We were coming out of the counter-culture/hippie era, but that didn't produce much of a political realignment as much as it began the leftist radicalization of the Democratic Party (more on that in a forthcoming chapter, too).

There was a major political realignment in America during that time, but it was actually the result of the civil rights movement, culminating with John F. Kennedy reaching out to Martin Luther King Jr. with "the phone call that changed history."[3] Although it seems odd to present-day political observers, from Reconstruction until Kennedy's call, blacks mostly voted Republican for decades.

Remember, the first-ever Republican president was Abraham Lincoln, known to history as the Great Emancipator. Democrats were the party of the KKK, Jim Crow, and segregation. They were personified by southern governors of that era like Arkansas's Orval Faubus and Alabama's George Wallace. Blacks couldn't officially attend the Democratic Party's conventions until 1924![4]

In fact, the legendary Jackie Robinson, who broke the color barrier in Major League Baseball, actually supported Republican Richard Nixon over Kennedy in the 1960 presidential election.[5]

But by 1974, the first post-*Roe v. Wade* election, the migration of black voters from the Republican to the Democratic Party was complete. It began with Harry Truman's reelection in 1948, when he received (then a record for a Democrat) 77 percent of the black vote after desegregating the armed forces. It was a major factor in his stunning upset of Thomas Dewey and has since resulted in Republicans never receiving more than 15 percent of the black vote in any election since 1964[6] (and often single digits).

After losing one of its core constituencies in the 1960s, Republicans were poised to lose the country in the 1970s.

Nixon had been reelected in 1972 by one of the largest landslides and popular vote margins in American history,[7] beating George McGovern, whose nomination was the first sign of the leftist takeover of the Democratic Party, by a whopping twenty-three points. He followed up his momentous victory by keeping a key campaign promise—signing the Paris Peace Accords to end the controversial Vietnam War just two months later.[8]

Nixon seemed to be bringing the country back together following the turbulent sixties, and was on his way to a historic presidency. It turned out his presidency was about to become historic, albeit not for the reasons he probably hoped.

A break-in at the Watergate Hotel, which seemed like a minor footnote to the 1972 election at the time, was about to break wide open and become the greatest political scandal in American history.[9] By October 1973, less than a year since Nixon's landslide win, his infamous "Saturday Night Massacre" put his presidency in unprecedented peril. He would manage to hold on to his office for ten more months before resigning in disgrace on August 8, 1974.

He was succeeded by his appointed, not elected, vice president and former congressman Gerald Ford. In an effort to move the country forward, President Ford pardoned Nixon of his crimes a month later. It had the exact opposite effect, instead enraging voters all the more.

Democrats surged to one of the biggest midterm election routs[10] in modern times, including adding almost fifty more seats to the majority they already held in the House of Representatives. This was in addition to winning several seats in the US Senate, and sweeping gains in statehouses across the country, too. Jimmy Carter would then defeat Ford for the presidency two years later, giving Democrats total control of Washington just four years after getting annihilated by Nixon.

The outlook was bleak for the Republican Party, which was also not coincidentally suffering from a serious identity crisis. Reagan, the former California governor who was once a Democrat, was urging the GOP to move to the right in response to the Democrats (and apparently the country) moving left. Party elders disagreed, prompting Reagan to challenge them in his famous "bold colors" speech and then challenge Ford for the 1976 nomination.[11]

As the 1980 election cycle drew closer, a series of gaffes, the hostage crisis in Iran, and an economy mired in a misery index made Carter vulnerable in his reelection—so vulnerable he would be challenged from the left for his party's nomination by Senator Ted Kennedy. Meanwhile, the GOP sensed an opportunity to reassert itself by seizing upon Carter's unpopularity, as a star-studded field emerged to vie for their nomination.

Among them was Reagan, looking to give it another go after falling just short in 1976. Except this time Reagan would have a new ally. It was a grassroots army that had never previously existed in the Republican Party and would go on to become the most feared, dreaded, and pivotal political constituency even in the present day. And it would've never been conceived without *Roe v. Wade.*

I'm referring to social conservatives, otherwise known as the Religious Right, Christian Right, Values Voters, Christian Coalition, or Scourge of Humanity (by its detractors in both parties), and so forth.

The constituency was forged by a previously impossible alliance of conservative Catholics and evangelical Protestants through the work of leaders like Paul Weyrich and Jerry Falwell (and others).[12] They discerned America was heading down a dangerous path of spiritual decline in the days since the sexual revolution, which was only cemented by *Roe v. Wade* and its escalating body count. This cultural sense of urgency motivated them to set aside serious theological differences, which had existed since the Reformation in the sixteenth century, in order to confront a common enemy—leftist secularization.

Keep in mind we were barely a decade removed from evangelicals being unwilling to vote for JFK out of fear he would follow the pope instead of the Constitution. Now they were aligning with Catholics to save the Constitution.

On the other hand, Catholics were just as wary of Protestants politically. While the Republicans were considered the WASP (white Anglo-Saxon Protestant) party in the early part of the twentieth century, America was importing masses of European immigrants, many of whom were Catholic.

These immigrant Catholics found a welcoming home in the Democratic Party and flexed their newfound political muscle in 1928, when Al Smith became the first Catholic to win a major party's presidential nomination.[13] They were a major reason why the Democratic Party's identity would be pro-immigrant, pro-middle/working class, and pro-labor for decades, until the leftists took over the party after the notoriously violent Chicago convention in 1968.

Prior to *Roe v. Wade*,[14] it was unthinkable that Catholics would majority vote for the WASP (Republican) Party. Nixon so dominated the overall electorate in 1972 that he became the first Republican to ever win Catholics. But to demonstrate how much of an outlier that was, consider Republicans (including the popular Dwight D. Eisenhower) only received an average of 34 percent of the Catholic vote in the five presidential elections before that.

Then came 1980.

With the Catholic Church already mobilized to confront the grave injustice of state-sanctioned baby murder, and joined by prominent Protestant pastors now marshaling those in the evangelical pews, a major political realignment was born. One whose impact is still felt in current elections, a generation later.

Reagan would have a three-pronged coalition (which would go on to be known as "Reagan's three-legged stool") his forerunner, Barry Goldwater, never had when he was crushed in 1964.

Economic and national defense/foreign policy conservatives would be joined by the social (Christian) conservatives. It would vault Reagan first to the nomination and then a decisive general election victory in 1980 over not just President Carter but a third-party candidate who threatened to siphon off enough base voters to play spoiler—liberal Republican John Anderson.

This history lesson was necessary to lay out for you the political clout pro-life voters bring to the table. There is no question there would've never been a movement/alliance of social conservatives without *Roe v. Wade*, and without that movement/alliance there would've never been a Reagan Revolution. It's certainly debatable whether Carter was so weak *any* Republican could've beaten him, but here's where the data wins again.

Reagan beat Carter by seven points among Catholics in 1980, according to exit polling. To prove that wasn't a fluke against an unpopular incumbent saddled by a struggling economy, Reagan would win Catholic voters by nine points according to exit polls of his 1984 reelection landslide. It began a trend that has carried forth through the most recent 2016 election as well.

*Whoever wins Catholics wins the presidency every time*, with the one exception being 2000, the year George W. Bush became a statistical anomaly by winning the Electoral College despite losing the popular vote.

Catholics have gone from being the most reliable Democratic voting bloc of the twentieth century to the ultimate swing vote of the twenty-first century. And that evolution was triggered by *Roe v. Wade*, the same event that triggered the formation of the "Moral Majority" within the previously politically dormant evangelical church, too.

Remember, Reagan was the first national figure in the Republican Party to prioritize the life issue and make it a central campaign theme. His primary challenge of Ford also resulted in its first mention in the official party platform in 1976.[15] By 1980, though, life wasn't just a plank but an entire section of the party platform. The only book published by a president while in office remains Reagan's *Abortion and the Conscience of the Nation* he released during his first term in 1983.[16]

Without the life issue on the table, Republicans historically have had little hope of capturing the important Catholic vote. And even with it, they still have to compete for it or risk losing it to the likes of Barack Obama and Bill Clinton. So maybe a Republican presidential nominee who wasn't as strong on life as Reagan was could've still beaten a weakened Carter, but history tells us it wasn't going to be a sure thing.

Which brings us to the present day.

As of the time I'm writing this book, majority Republicans in Congress are fully funding Planned Parenthood, an organization founded by a vehement racist[17] that is personally responsible for the deaths of at least seven million children[18] and has been caught on camera ghoulishly peddling dead baby parts for profit.[19] And yet, during the past twenty years when Republicans have been in control of Congress, they have heinously and inexcusably doubled Planned Parenthood's taxpayer funding.[20]

While I was writing this very chapter, Republicans handed Planned Parenthood,[21] the most prolific child executioner in American history, five hundred million dollars more of our money.

If the pure moral argument against funding such fiends doesn't move you, how about a purely pragmatic one? Planned Parenthood has long been one of the biggest financial benefactors for Democrats, spending at least thirty-eight million dollars to defeat Republicans nationwide in the last three elections alone.[22]

This begs the following question: What politician/political party in its right mind knowingly gives money to its opponents?

I think about this question at moments like I experienced during a pro-life speaking engagement I had in 2017. Before I gave the keynote speech, a local pro-life activist got up to urge the large crowd in attendance to get engaged at the state legislature. Her issue that was meeting resistance and struggling to get enough Republican support: voluntary pro-life license plates.

Stop and think about that for a second.

A Republican Party that was on life support, until pro-life voters gave it new life decades ago, has no hesitation about writing checks for hundreds of millions of dollars with our money for years to its opponents—who are literally Murder, Inc.

However, we have to scratch and claw to be lucky enough to get table scraps like license plates with pro-life slogans?

Such a feckless, treacherous enterprise doesn't deserve to live. But we have fought harder to keep this party of dry bones alive than we have for those dead babies. So alive the GOP remains while the killing continues.

# At Least We Can Hold the GOP Accountable

**TRUTH BOMB** *As long as the Democrats remain a hard-left, neo-Marxist political party, Republicans can get away with virtually anything.*

There's a largely ignored reason why the Second Amendment might be the only issue that we've moved the country to the right since Reagan left office.

The National Rifle Association and Gun Owners of America compete with each other for members. Though the NRA is superior in terms of its scope and total membership, Gun Owners of America has enough of a presence that the NRA cannot ignore them.

GOA is considered the more hard-core group by most observers, so the rivalry between the two usually plays out this way: If/when GOA goes too hard-core, the NRA is there to apply a defter touch. On the other hand, if/when the NRA seems too willing to deal for political expediency, GOA is there to hold them accountable.

One is the machete, the other a dagger. And different situations sometimes call for different weapons.

This is called a healthy competition. Healthy in that the competition between the NRA and GOA forces each to raise their game, keep it there, and the primary beneficiaries are always whom? That's right, the consumers, who in this case are those that want their Second Amendment rights protected and defended.

No other such dynamic exists within conservative issue advocacy. There is no national pro-life organization prominent enough to keep National Right to Life honest as it plays footsy with the Republican Party establishment.[1] While I was writing this chapter, I was contacted by a pro-life filmmaker to help him launch a viral campaign to pressure National Right to Life. Republican leadership in Congress was using the group's unwillingness to support "heartbeat legislation"—which says if a heartbeat can be detected, that's an obvious sign of life, and therefore the unborn child cannot be killed—as justification for not bringing it up for a vote.

I'm guessing just about every pro-lifer reading this is shocked to hear National Right to Life wouldn't instantly endorse such life-saving legislation, and are probably asking why. Well, there are lots of potential answers to your question—and exactly none of them are good. Furthermore, what if I were to tell you that in every conservative primary challenge to a GOP establishment incumbent in recent years I know of, National Right to Life sided with the establishment incumbent over the conservative?

Again, I know you want to know why, as do I. And, again, make sure you really do want to know why before asking, because the answers aren't likely to be comforting.

Conversations like this are a big reason why our issues get co-opted by the GOP, because too many of the organizations representing our issues get co-opted by the GOP, too. Once that happens, the issue becomes maintaining your seat at the Republican Party establishment's table—not so much the actual issue itself.

Yet one need not always become a sellout to succumb to this game. Sometimes our organizations/leaders submit to the Republican Party's shenanigans simply because the alternative is too unbearable to consider. And with Democrats essentially becoming the USA Communist Party, who can necessarily blame them?

If your perennial choice was getting stabbed in the back, which obviously hurts and may even cause paralysis, or being stabbed in the heart, which is obviously lethal, what would you choose?

Most people would take their chances on maiming than murder, while desperately wishing they had an alternative choice.

What's going on between Republicans and Democrats is the exact opposite of a healthy competition, which is proven by the inconvenient truth that the primary customers (who in this case are "we the people") are clearly not satisfied. Just take a look at voters' erratic behavior since we entered the twenty-first century.

In 2000, George W. Bush became the first candidate in over a hundred years to lose the overall popular vote but win the presidency. Further showing how divided the country was, the Senate was split 50-50, while Republicans held just a three-seat majority in the 435-seat House of Representatives.

In the 2002 midterms, voters then did something they'd only done three times since the Civil War (and never before for a Republican)—they gave more seats in Congress to the president's party. Voters followed up two years later in 2004 by reelecting

George W. Bush, and this time he won the popular vote, too. They gave Republicans four more seats in the Senate, and three more House seats as well.

But just when it seemed as if the American people were rallying to the Republicans, the 2006 midterms happened.

The same voters who had just unified behind the GOP swung completely the other way. Democrats captured thirty seats for control of the House of Representatives, making Nancy Pelosi the first female Speaker. And with so-called "independents" Bernie Sanders and Joe Lieberman caucusing with them, Democrats could also claim the majority in the Senate, too.

The tectonic shift continued in 2008, when Democrat Barack Obama crushed John McCain to capture the presidency. Democrats added another twenty-one House seats and swelled their ranks so much in the Senate they had a filibuster-proof supermajority there.

This means children born in the year 2000 saw the adults who conceived them totally reverse themselves politically before they completed the second grade! And the pendulum swings weren't done yet.

The Democrats would be annihilated in the 2010 midterms. Republicans gained a whopping sixty-three House seats, the biggest midterm election surge since 1938. They gained another six slots in the Senate and broke the Democrats' record from the 1974 Watergate election by adding 680 state legislative victories, too.

And then the American people followed up their anger at the Democrats by reelecting Obama president in 2012. And then the American people followed up their reaffirmation of Obama by awarding Republicans their largest majority in the House since

1928, along with the biggest midterm swing in Senate control since 1958.

By the time all the votes were counted in federal and state races, the 2014 election ended with more Republicans holding elected office nationwide since before the Great Depression.

Confused yet?

Let's throw in Donald Trump winning the presidency in 2016, with the strongest showing in the Electoral College by a Republican in almost thirty years (1988), despite losing the overall popular vote by almost *three million votes*. Oh, and did I mention that Trump won the Electoral College by a margin of less than eighty thousand *total* votes spread out over three states (Michigan, Pennsylvania, and Wisconsin)?[2]

And now those children born in 2000 saw the adults give full power in Washington to the Republicans, then the Democrats, and back to Republicans again *before they were eligible to vote for the first time* in the 2018 midterms. Speaking of which, the polling comparing voter enthusiasm among Republicans and Democrats six months before the 2018 midterm election was the exact opposite of what[3] it was in 2010. The numbers were precisely the same, only the polarity changed.

The American electorate has become the political equivalent of James McAvoy's lead character in M. Night Shyamalan's creepy hit *Split*, who has twenty-three different personalities. We are all over the place, except in this case I don't think it's clinical insanity like McAvoy's character suffers from as much as systemic frustration.

The American people like much of what the Republicans say and claim, and many of their talking points poll well—especially when they don't know they're what Republicans actually claim to think.[4] But they don't trust Republicans to follow through with actually doing what they promised once they're elected. After all, let us never forget this is the party that ran on fully repealing Obamacare for eight years, only to then not do it once they were empowered to do so.

On the other hand, the American people trust the Democrats are much more likely to do what they promised. But then they don't like it so much once Democrats follow through, and the budget-busting bill for their utopian schemes comes due.

In short, I could sum up all the polling on the two major parties I've ever been privy to in my entire career, either privately or publicly, with this statement:

> Voters don't trust Republicans and they don't like Democrats, which are their only two real options with no real competition for either on the horizon.

Other than that, everything's fine. We're all fine here. How are you?

Which brings us to the real culprit. The real reason for this voter schizophrenia, the electorate's wild mood swings, and our overall dissatisfaction with the never-ending two-party system.

The Democratic Party has surrendered itself to identity politics—otherwise known as cultural Marxism. This has driven Democrats to the hard left, making them the most extreme major political party in American history.

A thorough breakdown of the electorate by the Pew Research Center heading into the 2016 campaign cycle[5] tells the tale.

We have the highest percentage of registered independents in over seventy-five years. And Pew found that doesn't mean independents are by and large nonideological voters, as is often assumed, but typically they do lean one way or the other ideologically while preferring not to be identified with one party or the other (more on that below).

Pew found the strongest determiner of party affiliation in favor of Democrats was race or ethnicity. For example, Republicans held a modest nine-point advantage over Democrats among whites. But Democrats held commanding leads among blacks (sixty-nine points), Asians (forty-two points), and Hispanics (thirty points).

Meanwhile, religion was the biggest factor in your likelihood to be a registered Republican (except among Jews, where Democrats held a huge lead, but only about 2 percent of the US population is Jewish).[6] While it's true Republicans also dominate among married voters, keep in mind those who are serious about their religious faith are more likely to marry in the first place.[7] This explains why Republicans' lead among white evangelicals is forty-six points, which is thirty-seven points higher than its overall lead among whites.

Allow me to bottom line what this means in blunt language: people typically become Republicans *because of what they believe*, while people typically become Democrats *because of who they are*.

To put it in mathematical terms: one side advocating values as their identity + the other side using their identity *as the source* of its values = an extremely polarized electorate. And as a corollary, that's why I believe the group of people leaving both parties behind to become independents is growing. Which I know something about, because in the interest of full disclosure, I'm one of them.

It's not that we're all leaving our ideology behind as much as the tribalism too much of our polarized politics is reduced to.

Heck, I'm more right wing than ever. But nothing polarizes us more, or makes us more tribalistic, than identity politics.

Here's what I mean by that. When someone says "because of my belief in tolerance and diversity, and my rejection of Judeo-Christian norms as oppressive and exclusionary, I therefore believe in marriage equality," they are making a statement of values. You may not agree with their values, but this is a value that is a fulfillment of their ideology.

However, when someone says "because I'm same-sex attracted I should be able to marry someone of the same gender," they are asserting their identity as their value. Thus, if you disagree with them, you're not just someone with a dissenting ideology, but rather are discriminating against their identity.

At that point the debate ceases being about values, or maybe even being a debate at all. Instead it becomes a polemic about why you are a hateful, homophobic bigot in their eyes. And bigots don't deserve to be heard or have rights, of course.

When we disagree on values, even vehemently, we can still treat each other as human beings or accommodate dissent because we realize we're having an intellectual debate—even if passions are running high.

But when we disagree on identity, even politely, the temptation to dehumanize "the other" becomes too strong because it becomes an emotional debate. Thus, they take our intellectual dissent as a personal attack, no matter how winsome or courteous we are in communicating it.

This dark embrace of identity politics has made the Democrats a hard-left, neo-Marxist political party. It also explains why most of their responses to your disagreement with their ideology are a personal attack.

Didn't agree with Obama's economic policies, which resulted in putting more people on food stamps than the total population of Spain?[8] You're a racist.

Think every child deserves to have a mother and father? You're a homophobe.

Don't want to see millions of females slaughtered before they're born? You're a sexist or misogynist.

And on and on it goes. Furthermore, the reverb here is a son of a gun.

See, eventually we have these things called elections. And though in between them the Republicans we conservatives elected spend most of that time betraying, deceiving, and shunning us, sooner or later the first Tuesday in November arrives. And when we walk into the voting booth on that fateful day and stare down the list of would-be Marxists the Democrats have nominated, our resolve to finally tell the GOP to stick it where the sun doesn't shine withers.

Because this isn't your grandfather's Democratic Party. Heck, it's not even Bill Clinton's Democratic Party that still believed in balanced budgets, moving people from welfare to work, and religious freedom.

As I was putting the finishing touches on the original manuscript for this book in the spring of 2018, I couldn't believe how far left the Democratic Party was lurching. For example, back in 1995[9] every Democrat in the US Senate but one—former Klan leader Robert Byrd—voted to give authorization to move the US embassy in Israel from Tel Aviv to Jerusalem. However, when President Trump formally recognized the eternal city as Israel's true capital and officially moved our embassy to Jerusalem, *not one single Democrat showed up for the historic event.*

This came on the heels of Democrats siding with the ayatollahs in Iran[10] over our own president. Their congressional leader, Nancy Pelosi, openly admitted they planned to raise taxes at their first opportunity on an economy experiencing real growth for the first time since the housing market bubble burst back in 2008.[11] And they were even willing to go full gun grabber in an election year,[12] despite the fact the issue is *always* an election-year loser for the Left when they go there.

About six million people who voted for Obama in 2012 switched and voted for Trump in 2016.[13] And given how far left and anti-American the Democrats have become, there isn't a single reason for them to switch back.

I haven't voted straight-ticket Republican since 2004, but with Democrats making it plain they will attack every last morsel of our way of life if given the chance, I seriously flirted with going straight-ticket GOP in 2018 out of self-defense. At the same time, I was writing a book that also makes it plain conservatism has no future in the GOP! So believe me, I get why many of you reading this are willing to put up with *anything* the Republicans do to you. I'm susceptible to it, too. Who wouldn't be willing to tolerate almost *any* alternative to a loaded gun pointed at your head?

That's why we enable the Republicans once more, mainly out of fearful recognition of who the Democrats really are. We see what their true believers have done to our college campuses, our news media, and even the national anthem before pro football games. That's when we stare at the abyss, otherwise known as our ballot, and bite the bullet once more. I mean how many of you reading this right now have vowed never to vote for "the lesser of two evils" again, only to then do it again and again?

Well, let me love on you for a bit. I'm not here to condemn you. I *am* you. I've been where you are. And if not for a harsh lesson I learned in my childhood, I'd also be the dog returning to its own vomit Christ warned us about.

That is a harsh lesson I wouldn't wish on any of you, because it came from an abusive stepfather.

As I grew old enough to think for myself, my mom and I would often huddle after one of his violent outbursts. What would typically transpire is we'd trade arguments for or against leaving him. When one of us before had the gumption to go, the other would persuade otherwise, and vice versa. Usually that persuasive argument against going, and staying in the abusive relationship, was based on not believing we had anyplace else to go. We were stuck, and if nothing else he was a good provider.

In other words, he was better for our economy and the "lesser of two evils." Sound familiar?

I wish I could tell you that eventually we stood up to him, salvaged whatever dignity we had left, and kicked the dust off our sandals and moved on. But we didn't. That fear ruled us until he ejected on us—while my mom was recovering from a serious spinal injury and potentially looking at disability or worse. After she stayed faithful to him all those years, he bolted on her when she needed him most.

I promise you, unless we do something to change the current trajectory, this is how it will end for us and the GOP, too. It's already trending that way.

But there is a happy ending to our story. My mom eventually met another man, to whom she's still married, who has taken very good care of her for many years now. My children adore him as their grandfather.

## LIE #4

He was out there the whole time, just waiting to be found. Think about that.

# It's Too Hard to Start a New Party, So We're Stuck with the GOP

**TRUTH BØMB** *We're stuck with the GOP because there's too much money to be made by sticking with it.*

Three years ago, the Republican Party finally forced my hand.[1] So I left the party I had belonged to most of my adult life. The party I had volunteered and served several times since I was in high school. The party I've recruited and helped candidates for. The party of Ronald Reagan, my first political hero.

But to paraphrase some famous words Reagan once said, I didn't really leave the Republican Party. The Republican Party left me.

It long ago left conservatism behind. The betrayals we're seeing now on fake Obamacare repeals and Democrat budget priorities only confirm it. It's now leaving sanity behind, too, as it disintegrates into warring tribes of Absolute Always Trumpers and Absolute Never Trumpers.

Absolute Always Trumpers change their positions on vital issues like the Iran bribe...err...deal, despotic dictators, trade, and how much the character of our elected officials matter in order to conform to Trump.

Meanwhile, Absolute Never Trumpers can't ever seem to give the president credit even when he deserves it. I've even seen them argue against tax cuts and the Second Amendment, principles they've spent their prior careers advocating, in order to maintain their anti-Trump posture.

Each side of the Trump divide routinely clown themselves to justify themselves.

Then there's the so-called news. Much of it has devolved into shills for the Republican-Democrat duopoly now attacking that which they used to defend, and defending that which they used to attack.[2] This is on top of all the fake news peddlers on both sides, much of it driven by a desire to push narrative rather than report news. Thus, the preferred narrative *becomes the news*, with various platforms pushing confirmation bias for their audiences more so than presenting objectively true information.

A call I received recently from a producer at a major cable news network perfectly illustrates this point. He was prescreening my take on the day's controversy du jour, in consideration of inviting me on as a guest. When my take didn't conform to the traditional Republicrat Venn diagram, he politely passed on me by admitting, "We're looking for sides more so than opinions, if you know what I mean."

And yes, I know I already told that story. But I wanted to tell it again to drive this point home: it's clear it's time to try something new. The current political paradigm offers *no* hope for conservatism.

Of that there is no debate, except among those personally profiting off of maintaining this scam, and they are legion.

However, what is debatable is what to do next. And I believe this discussion needs to be conservatism's priority, rather than wasting another generation asking a political party to advance values they clearly don't share.

The way I see it, we have the following four options on the table for changing the paradigm (with pros and cons for each):

## 1. Hostile Takeover of the GOP

PROS: Why reinvent the wheel when there's already an existing major party in place with a conservative platform? Not to mention, while conservatives as a whole have little sway in the GOP, much of its rank and file are still conservatives. So why not marshal the grassroots' multitudes and truly take over the Republican Party? My 2014 book, *Rules for Patriots: How Conservatives Can Win Again* (which, again, this book is basically a prequel for), lays out a process for which that could potentially be successful. Another resource if you want to pursue this strategy is Richard Viguerie's book *Takeover: The 100-Year War for the Soul of the GOP and How Conservatives Can Finally Win It.*[3] Viguerie is referred to as the "funding father" of the conservative movement, because his grassroots fundraising techniques were considered revolutionary, fueling the efforts of many of those who signed the original Sharon Statement, considered to be the launch point of the modern conservative movement.[4]

CONS: Civil wars are long, expensive, and bloody conflicts. Do we truly have the resources for such a prolonged engagement, let alone the stomach for it? For example, for this to work would require exposing hypocrites and sellouts, which risks friendships and relationships. Not to mention it would also require raising at least eight figures in money, as well as current conservative officeholders to show a willingness to engage in hand-to-hand combat with party elders.

Even Ted Cruz and Mike Lee, arguably our two best US senators, have a policy of not endorsing against fellow GOP incumbents in contested primaries.[5]

Hence, if we had the onions (as college basketball broadcaster Bill Raftery likes to say), let alone means for such a civil war, it's unlikely we would've found ourselves in this precarious predicament within the Republican Party in the first place.

Heck, doesn't Viguerie's aforementioned book point out this battle has been going on for a century now? How many more years should we invest in a political party that clearly resists us and doesn't want us? After a while even Jesus says to kick the dust off your sandals and move on when you're repeatedly rejected by the same people, and he loved his enemies enough to die for them.

How do you fight for a political party that won't even fight for itself? As this book was being written, the GOP was getting destroyed in special elections that usually determine the trend line of the next election to come. Yet six months before the 2018 election, Speaker Paul Ryan announced his retirement, party leaders were already giving up on retaining the House and urging donors to focus on saving their slim Senate majority, and Republicans had no plans to pursue major legislation that would keep their unkept campaign promises.[6]

Democrat House Leader Nancy Pelosi's approval rating was fifteen points *worse*[7] than President's Trump's, which we're told each day is in the toilet and irredeemable by media in the tank for Democrats. So there's no reason whatsoever Republicans should just surrender the House of Representatives, and thus potentially sentence the country to a year of über-divisive impeachment politics in 2019.

*However, whether you think a team can still win the game or not doesn't matter nearly as much as whether they still think they can.*

Hence, when Republicans just leave the field with the fourth quarter still to play, it doesn't matter if the scoreboard says the game is still within reach. The outcome has been determined by their surrender.

If I were a cynic, I might say something like this:

They didn't fund Trump's wall. They didn't repeal Obamacare. They didn't defund Planned Parenthood. They didn't keep many of their campaign promises. But they did set up the Democrats to retake the House to impeach Trump, whom they also dislike (and they hate his base even more). So their work here is done.

Again, that's what I'd say if I were a cynic. At the very least, you can't want your political party to win more than they want to.

## 2. Bolster an Existing Third Party

PROS: Why reinvent the wheel when there are frameworks for existing third parties, like the Libertarian Party and the Constitution Party, already in place? Each of these alternatives already has a foothold in obtaining ballot access, which is considered the biggest challenge for any new political party. All they're lacking are numbers to take them to the next level, and there are enough of us to provide those numbers.

CONS: While there are factions of disenfranchised conservatives who will find much to like about the ideals of the Libertarian or Constitution parties, there are fundamental differences among them that could deepen existing divisions within conservatism. For example, the Constitution Party's platform explicitly states it acknowledges the religious premise of our founding fathers, and that premise is the basis for its beliefs.[8] However, the Libertarian Party's platform does not, but allows room for religious freedom within the context of individual liberty.[9] As the Proverb says: How can two walk together unless they are agreed? And let's not forget how the Libertarian Party failed to seize its moment in 2016 by nominating two former (and liberal) Republican governors for its ticket.

One final thing on this point, which is neither a pro nor a con but simply an observation. One that might be worthy of exploring further in another forum in the future. I'm going to briefly touch on it now, and you can flag it for later consumption if it becomes necessary.

While I don't believe either the Libertarian or Constitution parties could become singular alternatives to the GOP because of the worldview chasm, a tactical argument could be made that splintering into multiple offshoot political parties is the more strategic option. That instead of attempting to create a massive new vehicle with enough variance in its core worldview to accommodate substantial differences, which the Republican Party is already failing at, create multiple "wedge" parties instead.

Wedge parties are entities that couldn't grow large enough to replace the Republicrat duopoly, but could get enough people elected to drive a wedge through it. Meaning if you wanted to get something done in Washington, you would have to accommodate enough of the wedge parties' interests to have the votes. These are common in parliamentary systems nowadays, and it was how our political process worked until the post-Civil War era.[10]

For instance, let's say there was a specific "Pro-Life Party," and it was only two US senators out of a hundred from even small, rural, and pro-life states. If either Republicans or Democrats had a small-enough majority, like the scant two-seat Senate majority Republicans held in 2018, they would need the senators from the Pro-Life Party to pass much of their legislation. An argument could be made there's a better chance of defunding Planned Parenthood under that model than waiting another few decades for Republicans alone to finally do it.

Now, the wedge party strategy isn't foolproof. It's quite possible Republicans would just cease pretending to be conservative at all at that point and work even closer with Democrats to screw us. But if that's the biggest reason for not pursuing it, isn't that also an argument for not wasting any more of our time on the Republicans as well? Which leads me to the next option...

## 3. Create a New Party

PROS: A very wise man once said something about the foolishness of pouring new wine into old wineskins. After all, this country is a living example that once paradigms embrace corruption, independence from the corruption must be declared. Whether it is the Pilgrims fleeing from corruption on the *Mayflower* or the founding fathers loading their muskets to stand up to it, this is a universal truth of history: *puritans always end up becoming pilgrims.*

Never forget this. Corrupt systems/cultures/enterprises are *almost never* reformed once the corruption becomes fundamental to their very existence. This is why they will then turn on their own reformers, to the point of driving them out or even killing them in extreme circumstances.

That's why reformers (puritans) usually end up leaving, either voluntarily or involuntarily, and starting something new (becoming pilgrims). The notion that human endeavors so easily lose their virtue, and then typically fail to recover it once it's gone, was even discussed between founding fathers Thomas Jefferson and John Adams during their correspondence with one another in their later years.[11]

Once more, and I can't stress this enough and am confident Jefferson and Adams would agree: *puritans always end up becoming pilgrims.* Reform efforts rarely, if ever, work, and once the reformers realize the system loves the status quo just as it is, reformers will inevitably break away to form something new.

Therefore, as students of history, if we're going to spend years changing the paradigm, let's choose the strategy history says has the best chance of success: something new. Besides, wasn't the Republican Party itself originally founded by those who fled the stagnating corruption within its predecessor, the Whig Party?

*Never forget, there are only two reasons a politician will do what you want: they either agree with you or they're afraid of you.*

We long ago lost agreement with the mainline Republican Party, and now we're at the stage they no longer fear us, either. They would rather lose to Democrats than lose control to us. They fear backlash from the liberal media far more than backlash from the conservative base.

The GOP is not a child who won't be disciplined but one who *can't*. It's an ingrate party whose spirit animal is Esau, forsaking its birthright (conservatism) to feed its hunger today (donor-class dollars). Once a person or enterprise crosses that line, there's no turning back. You find yourself in a vicious cycle, devolving further to feed your frenzy, which only makes you more reliant on it.

In the case of the Republican Party, it has moved left to get the big money from its corporatist progressive donor class. In doing so, it abandoned its base, who no longer wishes to support it. Minus that base support, the party must keep slavishly doing the bidding of its progressive corporatist overlords to keep getting their money, which only further alienates it from its base. Thus creating a vicious cycle it cannot extricate itself from. Nor does it want to.

The GOP is not on crystal meth, which obviously and cruelly diminishes the appearance and faculties of those who succumb to it over time. Rather, it's on an opioid drip. The opioid is donor-class dollars, and as long as it can stop by the opium den (see that as K Street, where many of the big-money lobbyists reside in Washington) when it's stressed out and in need of a fix, it'll come out looking even more outwardly put together than it did going in.

The GOP isn't Chris Rock's ridiculous character from *I'm Gonna Git You Sucka*. Such a pathetic case will eventually hit rock bottom, which gives them a chance at a rebound. The Republican Party is more like the classic Pink Floyd song "Comfortably Numb." Yes, you may feel more than a little sick staying on the drug, but like any other addict, you can't envision letting the show (see that as another election) go on without partaking.

This party isn't a pathetic addict from the ghetto, but a sophisticated self-medicator from the Upper East Side. And you and I are never going to be able to compete with the high-class stash offered by the pushers on K Street.

CONS: This will require finding considerable resources that aren't currently identified, and until those resources are there there's little hope of raiding quality talent from the existing Republican-Democrat duopoly. For though many long for an alternative to it, their first priority is feeding their families. Of course, the reverse is also true, for without attracting real talent it becomes harder to identify those resources. The next largest expense is likely to be ballot access, and the two-party duopoly isn't prone to permit an unvarnished challenger to it without a costly court fight in that regard.

## 4. Reprioritize, Then Re-engage

PROS: An argument could certainly be made that the time, talent, and treasure that's been invested into partisan politics the past generation would've been better spent on church engagement and pop culture influence instead. In other words, go back to square one and realize the church is the institution most likely to produce the voters we're looking for. Then from there invest in influencing pop culture, because that's the most influential platform in America today. If the church is energized and pop culture is a platform for conservative ideals, the political parties will fall in line. As the late Andrew Breitbart used to say, "Politics flows downstream from culture."

CONS: This paradigm shift will require a paradigm shift in and of itself. For much of the church is either dormant, lacking the courage to engage, or considers becoming more like the culture we're called to confront "engagement," or if/when it does engage politically it does so more from a partisan rather than spiritual premise. Plus, conservatives have unfortunately been much better at condemning the leftist influence of pop culture than creating good quality pop culture ourselves. With the success of recent films like *I Can Only Imagine*[12] and others, perhaps that's beginning to change. Let's pray so. The harvest is plenty, but the workers are few.

* * * * *

I'm not what many would consider a major star within conservative media, therefore I'm hardly the one to lead this conversation or steer it one way or the other. And as you can see, there are pros and cons to each option. So I'm not trying to win an argument; I'm merely trying to start one—and a very necessary one at that. We must cease chasing our tail as a movement. See that as focusing on winning elections while the Left captures generations.

We need our leaders with mass followings to take over this conversation from here, because without them on board we'll likely continue to splinter—which means we'll continue to lose regardless of who wins in November.

So what's preventing that from happening?

Answering this question will bring this book to a pivot point, from which there's no turning back. From this time forward, if I haven't yet skewered your sacred cows, it's likely I'm going to. What it will require to finish this book from here, beginning with this question, will not ingratiate myself into the conservative clique. Quite the contrary, it risks my excommunication.

But I'm reminded of a phone conversation I had with former congresswoman Michele Bachmann toward the end of her 2012 presidential run. She had gone supernova, winning the Iowa Straw Poll in August to polling in the single digits by November.

It was an implosion of spectacular proportions. Maybe the greatest and most stunning in Iowa Caucus history. And she called me up to try and convince me to get off the sidelines and support her—I'd yet to endorse a candidate—in the hopes that might play some small role in helping her to reboot her scuffling campaign.

I told her that if she didn't think she could still win, there was no way I could help her do so. When she asked me what showing that she thinks she could still win would look like, I gave her this advice:

> You and your husband should huddle together and come up with a list of things you'd like to say to the country while you still have a voice they'll hear. While you still have a platform as a presidential candidate and congresswoman. Because the day may soon come when you won't have those platforms, so hold nothing back. Don't be sitting around ten years from now wishing you would've done this, or would've said that, when you had the platform and the chance. Go for broke. Go big or go home. This might be your last chance to stand up for what's right.

Bachmann would drop out of the race the day after finishing in sixth place in the Iowa Caucus with just over six thousand votes.[13] That's only about one thousand five hundred more votes than she had gotten while winning the Iowa Straw Poll five months prior.[14] Bachmann would then announce she would retire from Congress the next year, and she is now out of politics.[15] In just a few years she had gone from the new hotness in conservative politics to a nobody. The mob is fickle, and a society with a short attention span moves on quickly.

There's no reason the exact same thing couldn't happen to me, especially because I'm nowhere near the presence Bachmann was in her heyday. That's why I'm going to take my own advice with this book. Instead of looking at this as a career-builder, I'm going to write it as if it's a message-sender. A message I may only have a limited window to send before everyone else figures out I suck at this.

I literally came out of nowhere, thanks to a convergence of events I had nothing to do with that suddenly had me in the catbird's seat of a presidential election. So there's no reason I couldn't disappear just as suddenly. Let's face it, it's not like there aren't more talented, smarter, better looking, and wittier options out there. My platform could disappear faster than you can say "Scottie Hughes" for all I know.

Given there's a chance this may be my final opportunity to speak truth to power on behalf of my (and your) kids' futures, I'm going to take it. Here goes...

The reason we haven't taken over the Republican Party, formed a new party, or aren't even having a real conversation about how to do either one is the same:

*There is no money to be made doing so.*

A conversation I had several years ago with a member of the historic 1994 Republican takeover of Congress will drive this point home. He shared with me two of the examples that drove him from politics:

1. Like his peers in that historic 1994 class, he was drinking from a fire hose for months. Working insane hours to pass as much of the "Contract with America" as they could and keep their word to voters. One Sunday morning, he was reading an article in a major newspaper listing him as one of the top fundraisers in Congress, which perplexed him because he'd barely had time to head back home, let alone hit the fundraising circuit. So he did some checking around and discovered the culprit was the party itself, which was raising money off of him without his consent. The system simply couldn't resist cashing in on a rising star.

2. He also told me of a time when then-House Majority Leader Dick Armey wanted to reward social conservatives for helping Republicans gain power and offered them a key vote that had previously been unattainable. However, a couple of social conservative leaders—"names you would know," he said—then went to Armey behind closed doors to urge him not to hold the vote. "They wanted the issue politically," he said, "because they could raise money off it. I'm convinced that incident had a lot to do with why Armey has had a problem with Christian conservative leaders ever since."[16]

This brings me to the answer former congressman J. C. Watts gave me when I asked him why he went into self-imposed political retirement, right when he had become a conservative star:

I'm very thankful for what the civil rights movement did for black folks like me. Without that movement, there's no way a black kid like me could've become the starting quarterback at the University of Oklahoma. However, after college much of that same movement resented me when I became successful and started to think for myself. Instead of seeing me as a success story, it was almost like they acted as if they were better off if black folks like me failed. The civil rights movement had devolved from a movement to an industry. There was too much money to be made (in victimology) to move on and take advantage of our equality and successes. Now I've seen the same thing happen to conservatism. It's about selling books and selling out conferences more so than the issues. It's about personalities more than principles. Like the civil rights movement, conservatism has devolved from a movement to an industry.

Have you ever found it curious that Oprah Winfrey is considered the symbol of modern womanhood, despite the fact she has intentionally rejected becoming a wife and a mother—two of the most important and highest callings of womanhood? Seems counterintuitive, doesn't it? After all, since the vast majority of women will decide at some point to become moms and wives, how can Oprah possibly speak to their needs and life experiences when her life is nothing like theirs?

The same disconnect is happening within conservatism.

I don't care who you are, but wealth changes a person, especially great wealth. At the very least, it causes you to more insulate yourself from the masses, because the list of those who would love to take advantage of your success is as long as it is undistinguished. When you're especially wealthy, you're not as directly impacted by the Republicans considering raising the gas tax, as just one example. But many of the listeners/readers/viewers who made you that rich are.

What if you're unmarried, have no children, and/or living the jet-set lifestyle in Manhattan, Washington, or some other upscale place? How many of your listeners/readers/viewers are living similar lifestyles? How long does it take you living so much differently from your audience to cause you to lose touch with them?

The only reason why it's easy for us to assume celebrities like Oprah or some other leftist Hollywood figure are elitists, but conservative media superstars are somehow immune to this human condition, is because we don't agree with their politics. But elitism knows no political party, ideology, or viewpoint. It can happen to any of us when we conclude we have arrived and our feces no longer stinks.

That's especially true when we're mostly surrounded by others similarly afflicted, or we have made selfish lifestyle choices that allow us to live for ourselves.

A millennial conservative I work with, Chris Pandolfo, wrote an essay about our penchant to favor clicks over conservatism, and style over substance, as a movement/industry.[17] It was almost as if he were begging those of us in the elder generations to leave behind a conservatism worth his generation fighting for. I include his eloquent words here, and I pray we will take them to heart:

> Conservatives are perilously divided. Our movement has become driven by personality rather than by principle. Our leaders are fundraisers, managers, organizers, or hucksters— not statesmen. We are obsessed with the present and fail to put ourselves in perspective with the past and the future. And our movement is consumed by ambition, greed, and the self-serving desires of some to write the next vapid book and get the next shallow appearance on cable news, while others point, and scorn, and mock, and lecture from the ivory towers of their

own inflated egos. Stop this stupid, unproductive, worthless, tribalistic, fanboyish, clickservative culture of pitiful drama, vain one-upmanship, and holier-than-thou finger-wagging. Put aside this childish pro-Trump, anti-Trump, personality-driven egotistical flame war. While the conservative movement is distracted by nonsense, Americans are losing their liberty.

I wish I had this young man's maturity when I was his age. Heck, I wish I had it right now at my age, and I'm old enough to be his dad.

However, let us never forget all forms of prostitution are a two-pronged transaction. There is the giver and receiver, the hooker and the john. So if we're an industry masquerading as a movement, riddled with craven opportunists instead of earnest ideologues, such ne'er-do-wells can only cash in if there's an audience willing to purchase their services.

We have seen the enemy, and he is us.

# We Can Successfully Primary These Progressive Republicans

**TRUTH BOMB** *If you ain't got Fox News, Drudge, and Rush Limbaugh helping you take on the system, you've got nothin and you're wasting your time.*

I need to invoke a sage far wiser than I to confront this canard. So, ladies and gentlemen, without further ado, I present a man who needs no introduction when it comes to dropping some serious knowledge.

Of course, I could only be referring to Kenny Rogers, and perhaps the best counsel he ever gave—which admittedly is a lofty bar considering the esteemed source—is found in his classic song "Coward of the County." Which is an ode to the next generation, warning them not to repeat the mistakes of the previous one.

So much of this book is taken from my own personal and extensive experience in politics. Which is a nice way of saying I'm trying to help you learn from my failures, of which there are a treasure trove of lessons because there's been quite a few. In other words, I've lost—a lot.

Which, admittedly, makes me a loser, yes.

But also, therefore, a subject matter expert on how to win. Provided you're willing not to do the same mistakes I've done (and/or witnessed for that matter). One good way to become a winner is to do the opposite of losers like me.

That being said, this chapter, in particular, is a "Coward of the County" moment. Because if you're planning on launching and/or investing your time, talent, and treasure into primarying one of these progressive Republicans in Congress, I've got one piece of advice for you—*don't even bother.*

At least, don't even bother until you've checked to see if they're on the protected list of the three mighty gatekeepers, who really determine who does or does not get elected to national office in the Republican Party: Fox News, Drudge, and Rush Limbaugh (in that order).

These three represent the most powerful Republican triumvirate in politics since ancient Rome. They are where the vast majority of conservatives who vote in Republican Party primaries get their information. Thus, if they aren't mobilizing our base to storm the castle, you have as much chance of beating the GOP's corporatist progressive incumbent in a primary as I do of winning a Speedo model competition. So, like, slim to none— and slim is carbing up in the buffet line, going for seconds as we speak.

By the way, if you're not discouraged enough yet, now might also be a good time to let you know that the triumvirate almost *never* sounds the shofar against Team GOP. Which means you're on your own, kid. Which means you're dead on arrival and wasting your time because your biggest weapons are on self-imposed mothballs.

It's not that I'm trying to discourage you, but I'm trying to discourage you.

To discourage you from working hard when you should be working smart. To discourage you from tilting at windmills. To discourage you from getting your hopes up in believing there's some mass of conservative grassroots out there, just waiting for your principled champion to show up and offer an alternative to the local Swamp Thing come primary day. Oh, they're out there all right, but they won't even know your campaign exists without Fox News, Drudge, and Rush Limbaugh letting them know.

And if I've learned anything in electoral politics, I've learned this (and you neglect it at your own peril or receding hairline—whichever comes first): *the number one factor in determining who wins primary elections, and it's not even close, is name ID.*

Pardon me for a moment while I throw up in my mouth a little.

For some strange reason that seems to happen every time I acknowledge this most tragic of political realities. See, I was once like you, savagely pushing back on this sophomoric sentiment. Refusing to believe the gene pool was this shallow, especially on "our side." We aren't "low-information voters" like the Left. Our people care about actual substance and are always driven by logic and reason. They're not emotionally driven by #FakeNews and cults of personality.

Yeah, I used to believe stuff like that, too. Good times.

Then I worked for the 2016 Ted Cruz presidential campaign and witnessed moments like what happened during the final contested primary in Indiana. When every dimwitted inbred stereotype of uneducated flyover country "conservatives" ever aired on MSNBC actually came true. Don't believe me? Here's the link to the video.[1] Go and watch it for yourself right now. But I have to warn you, if you're not into cutting yourself currently, you will be after watching every *Daily Kos* polemic ever written materialize before your very eyes. Go ahead, I'll wait...

Welcome back. So that was a painful watch, huh?

Before I personally witnessed the dumbing down of America wasn't just for Democrats anymore, I also naively believed where a candidate stood on the issues, how they morally lived their lives, and how bad a RINO (Republican in Name Only) they were primarying actually mattered.

Oh, it does matter, just not on this earth.

Maybe on earth-2, somewhere else in the multiverse, or on the new heaven and new earth to come such important factors will matter. But on this earth, where all creation groans, most of the people are either lazy or uninformed. Or, if you're really lucky, uninformed *and* lazy. We are fulfilling *Idiocracy*—perhaps the most prophetic and among the most profane films of our era. As the film's narrator says:

> The years passed, and mankind became stupider at a frightening rate. Some had high hopes that genetic engineering would correct this trend in evolution, but sadly the greatest minds and resources were focused on conquering hair loss and prolonging erections.[2]

Sometimes this isn't our fault and we're earnestly busy. We'd like to be more mobilized and better informed, but life doesn't slow down so we can do more politics. We have families, churches, businesses, jobs, and so forth, that require our constant attention. We have a life to live, and for us politics isn't the be-all and end-all it is for the Marxist progressive, who elevates politics to a religion.

So we rely on sources we trust to essentially tell us what to think and/or do, like we rely on a trusted mechanic to tell us what's wrong with our car and how to fix it. For conservatives the Fox-Drudge-Rush triumvirate is, by far, the most trusted source. We can't fault those folks. They're doing the best they can to prioritize that which matters most in this world, and it's only natural that they would rely on sources and platforms they've made a life-changing amount of money for will return the favor by keeping them adequately informed and alerted.

And then sometimes, like they say in the movie *Office Space*, it's not that we're lazy, Bob, it's that we just don't care.

"I've been voting for [fill in the blank Swamp Thing] for so many years and he tells me he's a conservative so there" is basically the petulant battle cry of these Republican dhimmis, who think they're hard-core conservatives when really they're just useful idiots for the likes of Lindsey Graham. They're how a pearl-clutching progressive like Graham, who has proven he cares more about illegal aliens and fake Islamic "freedom fighters" than he does actual Americans, keeps getting reelected to the US Senate from a deep red state like South Carolina.

These are the people who think by mind-numbingly voting for the same progressive corporatist Republicans over and over again, regardless of better options being available, they're fighting for American exceptionalism. The exact opposite is true. Progressive Marxists ought to be sending these fools flowers, because they're doing more to help their cause than every episode of *The View* times ten.

The hardest sell in politics is to convince such partisan voters, who have been voting for an incumbent nominee over several cycles, to suddenly vote them out in a contested primary. Because it requires possessing two things tragically missing from the intellectual palette of many voters, regardless of their ideological persuasion: critical thinking and humility.

It takes critical thinking to spend at least as much time holding the Republican candidate, who claims to believe what you do, accountable to following through on those beliefs as you do cursing the Democrat, who doesn't even pretend to believe as you do. Unfortunately, too many Republican primary voters have what I used to call "little brother syndrome" when I worked in sports talk radio—meaning they are so driven by their hatred of their rival, they seem to get off more on their rival losing than they do their favorite team winning. Their favorite teams therefore become whomever beats their hated rival, and then—maybe—their actual favorite team. This impulse can be driven by the subconscious fear, which they will never dare vocally admit, that their rival may indeed be the superior competitor. Hence, "little brother syndrome."

Voters with little brother syndrome won't even look at where their partisan candidates stand on the issues in a primary. They'll simply vote for who they think is "electable." And usually "electable" is defined by people whose views are more closely aligned with Chairman Mao than Russell Kirk, of course. And if you try to force them to look at where partisan candidates in a primary stand on the issues, you will quickly learn what the Bible means by the term "stiff-necked."

They'll call you a "purist," as if striving for purity is somehow a bad thing, while also tacitly admitting that if you're for "purity," that means they're for "impurity." Thus hoisting themselves with their own petards. Which will never dawn on them, because critical thinking just ain't their jam.

They'll call you "unreasonable" or claim "you want the Democrats to win." To which you'll respond, "Hey, bro, this is South Carolina, not the People's Republic of Kalifornia. So why in the name of Sam Hill do we keep nominating a flaccid progressive like Lindsey Grahamnesty? When in this state we could nominate the Apostle Paul—and Romans 1 Saint Paul at that—and still get 55 percent statewide?"

That's when they'll call you a "theocrat" and start using the putdowns of conservatives with a conscience we usually read in the communist comments section over at the neo-Marxist Media Matters website, because "big tent" or something.

Often those who critically-think are accused of being arrogant by those who do not. The reality is a willingness to critically-think is the essence of humility, because it means you're willing to critique your own thinking/beliefs/opinions to see if they hold up to scrutiny. To put a finer point on it, you're willing to hold yourself accountable to the same standard you hold others.

On the other hand, self-righteousness is known by her children—and among her biggest brats is "I'll vote for the 'electable' candidate in the GOP primary" guy. Now, some of these people are just liars. Swamp Things and establishment shills who don't agree with us whatsoever. They're just using this talking point to deflect away from exposing their own fraud, knowing full well the mind-numbed are nothing if not dumb and haughty enough to lap it up like a litter of rabies-infested Pavlovian dogs.

I'm not talking about them. Don't get me wrong, I wouldn't urinate on these political hacks if they were on fire, yet I still respect them as a fellow combatant. We all gotta eat, and it ain't called the world's oldest profession for nothing. Hate the game, not the player, I always say.

However, I have no respect whatsoever for the "conservative" who falls for this con, because he does so willingly. He even brags about it. He's a dumbass traitor to his own cause, and he's totally proud of it, too.

We even have these quislings in the church. You can tell who they are by their favorite catchphrase when you call them on their horse puckey: "Well, I prayed about it, and I feel really good about where I am right now."

With God as my witness, these are the people in politics I struggle with not hating. Not the average Marxist progressive, who would have folks like me jailed if they could. Or at the very least put on a Homeland Security watch list. As much as I oppose where they're coming from, at least they're honest about the lies they believe.

But these so-called "conservatives" will smile to your face and then stab you in the back faster than you can say "potter's field." The only thing this ilk is good at is scoring touchdowns for the other team and calling it "pragmatism." The Republican Party is their cult. It's like they thank the chairman of the RNC, and not God, for the food on the dinner table each night. And if you dare demand Republicans behave like actual Republicans, they will excommunicate you.

This stiff-necked blind leading the blind are legion in Republican Party primaries. In fact, they are the *most likely to vote* in Republican primaries. Pouring into polling booths like a funeral procession from *Bleak House*, dutifully assuming the position for the corporatist progressives running the GOP—and thus

America—into the ground once more. In another time and place, they'd cast their babies into the fire for Molech, too, if they were convinced that was the demon who was going to win.

Some of you just winced at that, believing it to be too extreme. But is it really that much of a leap from genuflecting for Molech to voting for Republicans in a primary, who hand the baby killers at Planned Parenthood five hundred million dollars of your money,[3] when there is an actual pro-life alternative on the ballot?

As Barry Goldwater once famously said, "Extremism in the defense of liberty is no vice." When it comes to handing our hard-earned money to a private enterprise that dismembers and murders children for profit, a little extremism is called for if you ask me. The Scriptures say there are "six things the LORD hates." Among them are "hands that shed innocent blood." Maybe if we hated it, too, the so-called "pro-life politicians" we elect for Jesus would stop funding those blood-soaked money-grubbers?

Did I mention I struggle not to hate these people?

I'm not saying that's right; I'm just keeping it real. Like Martin Luther once prayed "Lord, curse Erasmus,"[4] these phonies make me want to get my imprecatory on. I know I should turn the other cheek, and deep down I really want to.

Like, I want to kick them really hard in one butt cheek, and then turn the other cheek and do the same to complete the butt whuppin'. Although something tells me that's not necessarily what Jesus meant by that expression.

But I prayed about it, and I feel really good about where I'm at right now.

I'm sure at least one of you thinks I'm being too harsh here, but this is again when facts become stubborn things. Like the fact Drudge didn't devote a single link to the tragic tale of Alfie Evans, the toddler the UK government did everything it could to starve to death in broad daylight, even though two different governments were willing to receive the child into their care. But he did link to a headline that read "Monkey Dressed as Blond Doll Forced to Beg in India" when Alfie needed him instead.

Like the fact of what happened in the 2014 US Senate primary in Kentucky, which was the moment I began to seriously consider for the first time we are utterly and undeniably toast.

That was the key race in the primary cycle when the Tea Party conservatives were supposedly going to primary the RINOs out of office, and the prime target was the prime RINO himself—Republican Senate Leader Mitch McConnell.

The consummate Swamp Thing, McConnell is exposed in the book *Secret Empires: How the American Political Class Hides Corruption and Enriches Family and Friends.*[5] It details how he managed to somehow *at least triple his net worth* while in public office on a public servant's salary. Hey, man, it's good work if you can get it, eh?

Nuggets like that make McConnell the Yoda of Swamp Things. He is a Jedi master when it comes to gaming the system all the while he's shanking us. Which justifiably made him our number one target that primary cycle.

And we lined up one heckuva candidate to go after him, too. So good of a candidate, in fact, that he—Matt Bevin—is now the governor of Kentucky! A self-made success story in the business world, whose family life and impeccable personal story are exactly what you're looking for to take out the likes of the feckless McConnell. One of my largest affiliates on the radio show I hosted at the time was in Louisville, so I covered this race almost every night on my program. And we had Bevin on several times as well. He was always on message, well spoken, and sharp.

Given how many times McConnell has betrayed us, and how good of a candidate Bevin was, this should've generated tons of media publicity to raise Bevin's name ID enough to make him a threat in a statewide election. And it did generate tons of media publicity—tons of mainstream/liberal media publicity.

In fact, I typed "Bevin-McConnell 2014" into Google just now, and eight of the top nine results that showed up were what mainstream/liberal media outlets like *Politico, USA Today*, MSNBC, and the *Daily Beast* wrote about that race at the time. Only one conservative outlet showed up—*RedState*.

Missing were, you guessed it, Fox/Drudge/Rush. And it doesn't matter if they show up beyond the first page of results, because like eight people in the whole flipping country ever go beyond page one's results when they Google something. And they're all shut-ins who claim to be anally probed in rundown trailer parks by gray aliens (and not of the illegal variety).

In fact, as I was writing this chapter just now, I went to FoxNews.com and typed "Bevin McConnell 2014" into its search engine. Zero—zero!—results came up. Which might explain why popular conservative commentator Erick Erickson said Fox News founder Roger Ailes, who was still running the network at that time, took him off the air because he was criticizing McConnell and McConnell didn't like that.[6]

"And it didn't matter why I was on television and on what topics I was or was not talking, [McConnell's wife] had told Roger I was an unwelcome presence on Fox and not a team player," Erickson said. "Roger had not only told me, but conveyed to my boss at *RedState* that I was becoming a problem for him with Elaine Chao [McConnell's wife]."

Needless to say, Fox would've provided us a huge boost to be rid of McConnell, but instead management at the time black-balled the one guy on the air who was actually speaking out about the race. And, according to Erickson, Ailes did it because McConnell's wife asked him to. Can you imagine what our reaction would be if we found out MSNBC took someone off the air because they were "an unwelcome presence" to Hillary or Obama?

Speaking of MSNBC, I went to its website and typed "Bevin McConnell 2014" into its search engine and received eighty-five results!

Unfortunately, most of our people aren't watching MSNBC or reading *Politico*, especially in a place like Kentucky, so it doesn't matter if they're literally doing GOTV for Bevin. It will gain a candidate like Bevin almost nothing in a partisan primary, because it does almost nothing to help him reach the demo most likely to vote for him. Which would be grassroots conservatives who don't trust *any* mainstream/liberal media (and for good reason), and thus get almost all of their information from the likes of Fox/Drudge/Rush. And they were giving Bevin no run at all.

What happens when his voters aren't even aware he's running to a candidate like Bevin, who again is now the governor of the state so he clearly wasn't some gap-toothed goober who can't string a sentence together? Numbers never lie.

First, let's set the stage here. Kentucky is a state Democrats haven't won in a presidential election this century,[7] and three times the Democratic presidential nominee didn't even get 40 percent statewide! Keep that in mind as I drop this bomb on you:

*The 2014 Democratic US Senate primary in Kentucky had higher voter turnout than the Bevin-McConnell race did.*[8]

And that's why Bevin didn't just lose; he got trounced.

"But Steve," some of you are saying, "I thought conservatives need low turnout primaries to win because our grassroots voters are the most likely to show up in a primary?"

Let me guess, you heard that from some RINO pundit on Fox News, right? Yeah, that's what I thought. Were his initials K. R. by any chance? I'm asking for a friend.

Take it from someone who's actually worked/assisted on campaigns, including several primary challenges of RINO incumbents—once again, compared to what you're being told, *the exact opposite is true.*

Again, it's the insipid "vote for the most electable" dhimmi Republican who's the most likely to vote in GOP primaries, otherwise known as McConnell's groupies/enablers, because our people often aren't engaged. And the reason they're often not engaged in the primaries is the outlets they trust the most to equip them to be—Fox/Drudge/Rush—for whatever reason(s) often don't call them to engagement.

Again, the numbers never lie, so let's look at the one primary the good guys won in the 2014 cycle—which almost nobody you know invested in because they thought there was no chance at victory. That would be Dave Brat's monumental upset over then-House Majority Leader Eric Cantor in Virginia. How did Brat do it?

The turnout *always* tells the tale.

Brat did not pull it off because Cantor's base stayed home thinking he had it in the bag, and so Brat rolled snake eyes on a one-in-a-million shot as the activists overwhelmed Cantor's larger but complacently overconfident base. Instead, Brat won because turnout *spiked a whopping 28 percent* from the 2012 primary Cantor won handily.[9]

And no, Democrats didn't cross over to take advantage of Virginia's open primary system (which the GOP establishment prefers, by the way) in order to deal a high-ranking Republican an embarrassing defeat. Rather, turnout spiked the most in the reddest counties in the district.

In other words, the grassroots conservatives showed up in droves, which Cantor's internal polling hadn't accounted for and shouldn't have—because they hadn't done so before. Except Brat seized on an issue our base cares greatly about—immigration—and that was the clarion call our base needed to show up for a primary they'd never previously participated in. The result was paradigm-shifting news, gentlemen.

Brat's victory shouldn't be an outlier, but a clarifier. One we seek to emulate nationwide by marshaling all our resources to do so, now that the template has been provided and proven.

And we could, if we had Fox/Drudge/Rush to help us rally the masses they've captured. But we don't, for whatever reason(s), so we can't. Which is good news for the McConnell family portfolio, bad news for the Constitution.

Hey, does anybody know what ultimately happened to that Indian monkey dressed up as a blond panhandler?

# LIE #7

# Principles Matter Most When Evaluating Our Candidates

**TRUTH BOMB** *A candidate's motivations and passions matter even more than their stated or professed principles.*

It's a meeting, usually over lunch, I've had so many times in my career. Sadly, more often than not it turns out the same.

It starts with the connection. Sometimes it's the pastor who reaches out, believing he has a promising potential candidate in his congregation looking for guidance on running for public office. Sometimes it's a reader/viewer/listener who contacts me and recommends I meet so-and-so who's saying all the right things. Every now and then it's the would-be candidate himself who initiates the relationship.

Very, very seldom will I initiate, because I've found every single time I've sought the candidate out they have turned out to be disappointments. After all, when you have the ability to help someone accomplish their goal, but they don't seek you out to obtain that help, that probably means one of two things: either they're too lazy/incompetent to deserve the office, or they're not who they're claiming to be and don't want to risk my exposing they're counterfeit.

Once the connection is made, the meeting takes place. We sit down, exchange pleasantries, and find common ground on sports or movies. Then we start talking theology and it's like we share a brain. Even on areas we have a different take it's clear there's a common interest there. So far, so good.

The conversation then transitions from general theology to the political philosophy it gives birth to. We may not agree on each and every point, but why major in the minors when we agree on the most important things? From there I come away excited and offer to help. Usually that means making a call or two to people I know with influence/resources that can make a difference in their campaign. If they're decent-enough communicators I may give them free airtime to help with their exposure. If requested and I really believe in the candidate, I might even work for and/or consult with them on the side. But I'm like a vampire—you have to invite me in on that level.

Sometimes we win, sometimes we don't. Most of the time it's not the ones you lost that bother you, unless it was truly a *special* candidate. Not a good one, but a *special* one. Otherwise, you take your lumps and get yourself out of bed the next morning. Life is full of disappointment, unless you're Joel Osteen apparently.

*It's the ones you win now, and then lose later, that sting.*

They always leave a mark. Maybe even a permanent scar, because you feel as if you were duped and you should've seen it coming. That you aided and abetted your own betrayal, and thus the betrayal of your audience. You'll beat yourself up something fierce internally asking questions like, "How could I have missed _____ that should've warned me this guy was gonna turn on us once in office?"

This has happened so many times I've lost count. Two recent examples come to mind, because they're both still in elected office in Washington.

To help promote the release of my previous book, *Rules for Patriots: How Conservatives Can Win Again*, I spoke at an exclusive gathering of conservative leaders called the Council for National Policy (often referred to as CNP for short). This is a who's who of conservative movers and shakers, and it's by invitation only.

Your initial invite usually requires you to be sponsored by an existing member. It's also not cheap to go, because it's usually at a five-star hotel for the weekend. But if you can swing an invitation and the cost, it's a great place to go and network, yes, but also to get refreshed/equipped by other conservative thinkers/leaders. And there's only four a year, so there's limited opportunity to engage such an esteemed group.

Needless to say, CNP was an ideal place for that book's message. Every kind of potential or actual leader is in attendance—prominent organizational heads, pundits, media stars, candidates, elected officials, donors, and so forth. So when I was invited to do a book signing there I jumped at the chance.

After my panel concluded, the book signing was held right outside the ballroom. One of the first people waiting in line to meet me was a man named Barry Loudermilk. He is now the congressman from Georgia's Eleventh District, which is so Republican he didn't have a Democratic opponent in the general election after winning the 2014 primary,[1] and got 67 percent of the vote against his Democratic opponent in 2016.

In other words, unless it turns out Loudermilk is a capo for El Chapo, he couldn't possibly lose his seat in a district like that. And even if it turned out he was a cold-blooded assassin for one of the planet's worst drug lords, Democrats would at best still have a 50-50 shot of flipping his district.

But the day Loudermilk sought me out, he wasn't a congressman yet. He was still trying to fend off former congressman Bob Barr in the runoff election to come, which would decide the party's nominee and thus the election. Because Loudermilk had become a grassroots favorite, I knew who he was. And I was pleased he had watched my panel, and then came to talk to me more about the book. In my mind I wrote it for patriots just like him, so they could take on the system, fight, and win. And not just on Election Day, but on public policy once in office—when it matters most.

Loudermilk seemed right out of central casting: a veteran who served in the Air Force, a graduate of a Baptist university, and he'd already built a conservative record in the state legislature so he wasn't an unknown. Based on bio alone, Loudermilk seemed like the archetype of what we're looking for.

We spoke at length about the book's observations he agreed with, the state of the Republican Party in particular and culture at large, and how to take on the system once he got to Washington. I remember coming away thinking we're going to be hearing a lot more from him in the future. We seemed like kindred spirits. He even gave me his card with his personal info so we could stay in touch.

Almost five years later, though, and Loudermilk is basically in the witness protection program. It's like he never even got elected. As of this writing, his Liberty Score is a pathetically mediocre 72 percent (C-minus)[2] even though he represents a 100 percent district. He's taken on no fights I know of. He didn't join the Freedom Caucus, which is at least trying to do something, anything, that conservatives care about.[3]

There's literally no point in Loudermilk being there from our perspective. There's a bunch of corporatist progressive Republicans, who didn't rally around the flag in the military or graduate from a conservative seminary, who could've mustered up a C-minus congressman from such a conservative district. And now Loudermilk will likely hold that seat for as long as he keeps his nose clean. Giving us meaningless mediocrity from a district that should've sent us a conservative difference-maker.

If only Loudermilk's story were unique, but it's not—it's legion. Here's another one from my own backyard. Her name is Senator Joni Ernst.

In 2014, we had a rarity in Iowa—an open US Senate seat with Tom Harkin's retirement. That gave Republicans their best chance in years to capture the slot opposite Senator for Life Chuck Grassley. However, early on the slate of candidates had failed to inspire the primary electorate. I waited until the field was completed before engaging the process, and then began meeting with several of the candidates to see where they were and to consider supporting any of them.

I already knew all the candidates vying for the conservative vote in the primary except for one, Ernst, whom I had yet to meet since she got elected to the state senate. Her initial US Senate campaign had gotten off to such a rocky start, the party establishment was urging her to drop out of that primary and run for the House of Representatives instead.

She agreed to meet me at a coffee shop in downtown Des Moines, where we discussed the status of her campaign, which was frankly in dire straits at that point. Like Loudermilk, Ernst was a proud veteran who had built up a pretty conservative record in the state legislature, especially on my most important issue: life. She really sold me on her conservative convictions in that meeting, and I remember walking out of there mystified she wasn't performing better as a candidate.

I even reported back to some prominent conservative influencers afterward to keep their eye on her. She was underrated, I said, and contrary to conventional wisdom, if she could land on a message she wasn't done for given the status of the field. Not to mention, Iowa Republicans were eager to be responsible for the state's first female senator.

It was just a matter of weeks later when Ernst would find that winning message, when she released one of the greatest political ads in my state's history. An ad that went viral and made her the talk of the political world. It was simply titled[4] "Squeal," but the message therein was profound. It perfectly captured the anti-Washington fervor sweeping the country, with Ernst vowing to make Washington's money changers squeal like a farm pig about to be slaughtered or castrated.

It vaulted her from afterthought to front-runner in a matter of days.

I would next see Ernst about six weeks after the ad's release at a GOP Senate primary debate. I was blown away at her performance, and not in a good way.

It's like she had become a completely different person from the one I met at that coffee shop. Her answers were so canned she seemed programmed. She was more artificial intelligence than human being. She wasn't even a pandering politician, but a platform for the spewing of clichés. It was like watching a life model decoy in real time.

# LIE #7

I thought there was no way the woman on that stage was going to win the primary, but to the majority of primary voters she wasn't that woman on the stage. She was the badass who was going to make Washington insiders squeal—all thanks to that viral ad that made her name ID explode. So she could've squealed like a stuck hog herself on the stage that night, and it wasn't going to change the eventual outcome on primary day one iota. The die was cast thanks to some slick marketing.

I had to go to Washington, DC, a couple of weeks later for some meetings, and wherever I went inside the Beltway, when people found out I was from Iowa all they wanted to talk about was Ernst. She had become a rock star in a town she had gotten famous threatening, which in hindsight probably should've been a sign to me they knew she wasn't really serious. But this was a shtick to win over the gullible plebeians. If anybody knows a scam when they see one, it's Washington.

Real recognizes real.

I didn't see Ernst again until after she convincingly won the primary with no ground game to speak of. Just a pure rout based on name ID alone, all thanks to that viral ad. Later that summer, when I saw her at the biggest annual gathering of pro-lifers in Iowa, we asked her to sign a petition to urge the Iowa legislature to pursue language that defined life as beginning at conception.

She refused, telling us she feared it would be used against her as too extreme by Democrats in the general election, *despite the fact Ernst had already co-sponsored that exact same legislation in the state senate.* Ernst had already gone from promising conservatives to make the system squeal to squealing in fear of the system herself, and she hadn't even been elected yet.

Now, that's what I call hacktastic!

At the time I'm writing this, Ernst has a robust 63 percent Liberty Score (sucky D-minus).[5] That doesn't so much say "drain the swamp" as it does "lied right to your face." But I'm one of those silly people who still expects folks to follow through on what they promised me. I should probably give that up for Lent next year.

The reason I was fooled by Loudermilk and Ernst, and by several others over the years, is I kept making the same mistake. A mistake many of you reading this are making as well. I didn't learn, until it was too late, that before I grilled them on the issues I needed to discern something even more important than their beliefs.

*I needed to discern their motivations and passions.*

See, it's not ideology that ultimately determines how faithfully an elected official will honor their oath of office, but their ambitions. What's truly driving them to seek public office in the first place. *All* politicians can be broken down into two categories, and it's not conservative versus liberal, Republican versus Democrat, or even grassroots versus establishment. It's a far more basic instinct than that.

*Are they running to do something or be somebody?*

If you end up finishing this book, you will have read thousands upon thousands of words, but those nine words I just typed in italics are among the most important I'll write. Don't ever forget them. Take them to heart. Make them a "trusty saying" as Saint Paul would say. Share them with everyone you know.

Those who are running to do something are comfortable in their own skin, even if they're a little socially awkward in their own skin. Because our partnering with them on a common cause, which they believe will preserve liberty and empower American exceptionalism, means more than whether or not we're gonna be buddies.

However, those running to be somebody will reinvent themselves at the drop of a hat—or better yet the advice of a single consultant. They're trying to connect with you more than convince you, since they have no real convictions to begin with.

They have no real reason for running other than the desire to win, the quest for power/prestige, or someone with power/prestige recruited them to basically be their political equivalent of a ventriloquist dummy. They see that as the candidate has crap for brains, so when their den mothers shove their hands up their rectums they control what they say.

The problem is too many of us want a buddy more than a champion, so we're constantly snookered by the opportunists running to be somebody. We'll even sabotage those running to do something in our primaries, convinced they're not likable enough to win a general election.

*Elle* once published an article criticizing Senator Rand Paul for his odd hairdo, referring to him as "Strand Paul."[6] Not to mention the diminutive Paul arguably has even less charisma than his quirky father.

But while I don't agree with him on everything, we'd be far better off as a nation if we had more senators like Paul than Ernst. So why don't we? Do you really want to know? Do you really want me to answer that one?

Forget about it, I'm going to answer it whether you want me to or not—because you need to hear it nonetheless.

The reason we have far more elected officials like the zombified, cliché-spewing life model decoy Joni Ernst than the socially awkward substantive ideologue Rand Paul is because one is a reflection of who most of us are and the other is not.

Can you guess which is which?

# It's All About the Party Platform

**TRUTH BOMB** *The party platform is irrelevant to almost every Republican you elect.*

Stop me if you've heard this one before: "I'm not voting for the candidate, I'm voting for the platform."

Heck, not only have I heard this one before, and still do often—I used to say it myself. Now that I've gone through tribalistic detox, I realize how profoundly silly this talking point sounds. I mean, what kind of woman responds to her parents, when confronted with the obvious evidence the man she's about to marry is a complete cad, by saying "I'm not marrying [so-and-so], I'm marrying a husband."

A woman isn't marrying an ideal or an institution—she's marrying a man. And that man has an established character it's her job to know before deciding to endorse it by saying yes to his proposal. Similarly, you and I are not voting for a party platform—we are voting for people. And each of these people has an established character it's our job to know before deciding to endorse them with our vote on Election Day.

However, as conservatives, while we may champion the individual in our policy preferences, politically we tend to see things as a collective. Since, as I established in a previous chapter, most people become Republicans because of what they believe, we see the party platform as some kind of Mosaic derivative. Almost as if right after Moses handed the Israelites the stone tablets, a *Reader's Digest* version was compiled for the Republican Party platform still to come.

As a result, the good news is the modern Republican Party platform is a highly moral, ethical, and constitutional enterprise. The bad news is it's basically irrelevant in the grand scheme of things. Despite all the painstaking time and effort put into compiling it, on any given day it has precisely *nothing* to do with the policy outcomes—regardless of the outcome of the previous election. Worse yet, it's not even a consideration. Once it gets published it's like it doesn't even exist.

To the average conservative, the GOP platform is a mission statement. But to the average GOP elected official it's a nothing burger.

If you would've told me when I was first starting out in full-time activism that I would ever say such a thing, I would've had your mouth washed out with soap. Or, someone would've had to do that to me as punishment for all the bad words that would've come forth. But then I met a guy named Stew Iverson.

I was entering the peak of my influence on my statewide radio show, when two people who I thought were conservatives (one of them actually was; the other turned out to be perhaps the most dishonest person I've ever met in this business) came to me asking for my help getting elected to our state's Republican National Committeeman/Committeewoman.

While these are largely ceremonial positions policy-wise, it can still be quite valuable to have the like-minded in these posts.

That way they can report back home what's truly happening at the national party level to hold them accountable.

I had already learned the lesson that it wasn't my extra special ability to articulate eloquently my views that gave me influence, as my ego preferred, but rather the realization that via the show I could provide sunlight to what was happening in the shadows. Remember what you learned from Lie #6: the biggest problem we have is our base is uninformed about how they're getting screwed until it's too late (if at all). I was regularly sounding the shofar to hold these Republicans accountable to their base (who they don't like and/or agree with), and that's why they loathed me.

For if there's one thing every hacktastic politician hates, it's accountability.

So when this duo came to me about helping them, I was all ears, because I figured they would be conduits to helping me keep the audience informed and therefore active. They told me a guy named Stew Iverson, a former moderate Iowa state senator who was now chairman of the Republican Party of Iowa, stood in the way of their ascendancy. So I came up with one of my rare good ideas.

Instead of having these two on by themselves to promote their candidacy prior to the state party convention, I would invite Iverson to come on with them.

If Iverson declined to come on, which I assumed he would because most party hacks do, the audience wouldn't mind listening to us club him for an hour. Since we offered him the chance to speak for himself, and he revealed himself to be a coward, the audience wouldn't consider us to be unfair. If there's one thing *every* conservative hates, it's a coward. On the other hand, if he did agree to come on, he was outnumbered and there was no way he could win the exchange.

In other words, he was cornered either way.

To my amazement, or maybe it was glee, Iverson actually agreed to come on, proving while he wasn't a coward, he also wasn't very smart. Then again, he didn't really have much of a choice if you think about it, so he chose what he thought was the lesser of two evils. See what I did there?

The conversation that afternoon was going as expected at first. I got out of the way and let the conservative duo confront Iverson. Since I was giving them a chance to attack Iverson from the right, which mainstream media almost never lets us do, they were repeatedly pulling his pants down. I really hadn't said much at all up until this point, which was my plan going in.

But then something happened that I still have Iowa activists bringing up to me, so many years later. Something I didn't intend to happen. But the sun doesn't intend to melt vampires into oblivion, either. It's simply the natural byproduct of what happens to a creature of darkness.

A conversation about the party platform came up as they were arguing. Specifically, it was the life issue (the woman running for National Committeewoman was our state's leading pro-life activist at the time), which in Iowa (as it is in many other states) was the number one plank in the GOP platform. To my surprise, Iverson seemed ignorant of that fact as he was advocating against putting "purists"—see that as those who actually have conservative principles—in leadership positions within the party.

You know, "big tent" and all that.

As I was listening to a stream of horse puckey spew forth from Iverson's pie hole, I finally inserted myself into the conversation with what I thought was a flippant, snotty aside. You know, like basically most of my commentary is.

"You act like you haven't even read the party platform," I sarcastically said to Iverson, my state's Republican Party chairman.

That comment seemed like truth serum that threw Iverson off his stride, and for the first time he departed from his talking points to reply, "I haven't read it."

I remember that comment lingering there for what seemed like a William Shatner pregnant pause. I was speechless for at least two seconds, which admittedly is a lot for me. But I needed to run what just happened back through in my mind. Did my state party chairman just admit to the state's largest audience of conservatives he had so little regard for the principles his party's supposed to stand for that he hadn't even read them?

"Wait a minute, you haven't even read the party platform?" I asked incredulously.

It was then I saw Iverson sink further into his studio chair, knowing he had committed a (major) gaffe—see that as when a phony hack opens his mouth and the unvarnished truth comes out—that he now couldn't take back. So he repeated it once more, and then I frankly don't know what he said next as he tried to clumsily own it. Making it sound like he had more pressing matters than to know the explicitly stated principles of the organization he was charged to lead.

And it really didn't matter what he was saying now, because no one else would remember it, either. His goose was cooked, and at the upcoming party convention the two conservative challengers were elected by the delegates over his wishes.

The clip of Iverson's gaffe ran as a promo for my show for quite a while. People shared it in the early years of social media.

Iowa conservatives would email me for requests of the clip so they could share it with other activists who didn't believe it, which I technically wasn't supposed to provide but I did anyway. Iverson never really lived it down. He would be replaced as state party chairman soon after.

The real reason Iverson's gaffe was so potent was because we all knew it wasn't a one-off, but an admission of the only thing that truly made sense, which we always suspected but didn't want to have to admit to ourselves.

This party doesn't give a rip about us.

As we say on my show, "Occam's razor is always in effect." In other words, the simplest explanation, or the one that requires the fewest amount of assumptions to justify, is usually true. And while it may be painful to admit you're voluntarily submitting to leadership from feckless betrayers who wouldn't pee on you if you were on fire, that doesn't mean it's not true.

Lots of things in life that are painful to admit are true. Like when my wife asks me all the time now, "Is something wrong? What's with that look on your face?"

To which I'm forced to painfully admit, "There's nothing wrong; that's just my face. That's what I look like now."

There's a reason they say, "the truth hurts." There's a reason Jesus Christ, who loved us enough to die for us while we were cursing him, refers to the truth as a "double-edged sword." There's a reason why utilitarian ethics—which emphasizes pain avoidance as an alternative to virtuous suffering—is all the rage these postmodern days.

The truth is not our natural habitat as a species. We prefer lies, and the prettier and the littler they are the better. That's probably why a series called *Pretty Little Liars* was perhaps the most popular show on a cable network few people can even name (Freeform).[1] More people watched that show than any of the prime-time shows on CNN. There's a joke there, I know, but as Darth Vader once said, "All too easy."

See, the truth is something we must *submit* to, and we've all got this voice inside each of us telling us submission is bad. Unless we can make others submit to us, of course; then it's actually quite dandy. Submission to me but not to thee.

If you're a committed conservative, you embrace truth on some level. As I said way back at the beginning of this book, conservatism isn't an ideology as much as it's an observational science. Conservatives are those seeking to conserve that which history has revealed to be what's best for mankind. To put it even plainer, conservatives believe truth exists, desires to be found, and must be conformed to in order to conserve what's good and just for this and future generations.

The Republican Party platform, crafted by committed conservatives nationwide, is a written reflection of this worthy mission. However, while it may be the manifestation of what committed conservatives believe, it is not reflective of what most elected Republicans believe whatsoever.

And that's at least partially our own fault.

Come now—let us reason together; we're all conservatives here. As a general rule, we reject victimology. So while the soullessness of our politicians isn't our fault, our penchant for making ourselves routinely vulnerable to it is.

There is no perfect antidote to scam artists while we remain east of Eden, but with the right remedy we can make ourselves much less exposed to them. It's similar to how there is no cure for the common cold, but basic hygiene like regularly washing your hands makes you less prone to it. And yes, there's a reason I compared our dealings with the Republicans to washing the sickness-causing germs off our bodies. They're that foul.

That remedy is discerning a candidate's *convictions* instead of their *positions*.

A conviction is something that comes from your core, shapes who you are, and therefore couldn't be defied if you tried. Like when you're driving down the freeway and someone cuts you off, nearly running you off the road. You may really want to run them down and then run them off the road in retaliation—until your conviction against unjustifiably taking a life kicks in, and your conscience thankfully gets the better of you.

Convictions are the hills you're willing to die on, and in politics *you're always the hills you're willing to die on*. Any politician who isn't willing to die on the same hills you are isn't with you, regardless of what they claim to the contrary.

A position is something you shape when it's convenient and expedient for you. Like you may claim to believe in marriage as an institution until it's no longer convenient or expedient for you to be married.

I don't mean when there's been a betrayal, or one spouse is a physical threat to the other and/or the children. I mean when you've "grown apart" or "fallen out of love," so it's time to find a better provider, someone more sexually compatible, or someone you find more attractive. In those instances, your belief in the institution of marriage is not a conviction but a position. One you verbalized during your wedding vows, and maybe even passionately and sincerely at the time, but departed from once your basic instinct conquered your conscience.

We ask our candidates their positions, such as if they are pro-life, low-tax, and strong national defense. But they can be trained by consultants to say certain buzzwords or catchphrases to align with our positions. Or they can even have those positions for real on the campaign trail, until they get into office and realize those positions come with a price they're not willing to pay. Then they're gone with the wind, dude.

Here's a trusty guide to help you discern a candidate's real convictions on four of our most important contemporary issues:

## Life

Instead of asking them if they're pro-life, ask them when they think human life begins. If they say anything other than conception (or biological beginning), they're not really pro-life. And if they say conception, then ask them what they plan on doing to protect life at conception, as well as what they've done up until this point. If they've got no answer to protecting life at conception, or they have exceptions other than when another life is at stake, they're not really pro-life. They may be anti-abortion, as in they oppose abortion on demand as a barbaric practice, but they're not really pro-life.

*And I can promise you this: a candidate who won't protect the God-given right to life won't protect any of your other God-given rights, either.*

So always start here. Life is more than a litmus test, but a window to the soul. If they fail here, there's no point in continuing the conversation.

## Taxes and Spending

Instead of asking them if they're for tax cuts or a balanced budget amendment, ask them if they think taxation is primarily a moral or economic exercise. Also ask them what's the primary role of government in our lives. If all they offer is economic mumbo jumbo, or more contrived talking points about reining in spending, then at best they are technocrats who can't be trusted to hold the line on your money when "something must be done." At worst they are flat-out whores who will come hither once the progressive corporatist leviathan rattles its zipper.

## National Defense

Instead of asking if they believe in a strong national defense or interventionism, if they're a neo-con, or can repeat "like Reagan, I believe in peace through strength" just like they rehearsed with their consultants, ask them what they believe our role in the world is. Do we have the responsibility to enforce human rights, and what are those anyway? How would we know when our strategic national interests are at stake? When does a president require congressional authorization for military action? What does victory look like?

After President Trump bombed Syria (again) for gruesomely gassing its people (again), I asked the following questions:

1. How did Qatar go from our ally versus Iraq to an adversary that promotes Al-Jazeera and terrorist propaganda?
2. If bombing Bashar al-Assad (Syria's dictator) was a deterrent to him gassing his people, why didn't it work the last time we bombed him?

3. How come we allowed Turkey, whose president puts a sympathetic, mainstream front on Islamic radicalism, into NATO?

4. Why aren't there any Christian churches in Afghanistan?

5. Why was last year the deadliest year yet for civilians in Afghanistan?

6. Why did we invade Iraq only to allow it to become a proxy state of Iran?

7. Why did our former secretary of state side with Qatar over Saudi Arabia last year, when the Saudis attempted to come down on Qatar for cozying up to Islamo-fascists?

8. How come we were on the wrong side of the Arab Spring in Egypt and Libya?

9. Why doesn't Israel have to occupy these Muslim lands to protect itself?

10. If we are going to practice interventionism, then why didn't we do anything to promote/assist the demonstrations against the ayatollahs in Iran last winter?

11. Why have we repeatedly abandoned the Kurds, who have been on our side for decades now?

12. What does victory look like? (We can't ask this enough if you ask me.) For example, we're now focused on fighting ISIS, which didn't come into existence until more than a *decade* after we launched the war on terror after 9/11.

13. Why have these people with similar religious and moral customs, common ancestry, and so forth, been killing each other since a thousand years before the Pilgrims landed at Plymouth Rock?

I realize this line of questioning is more thorough and detailed than most of you probably think you have free time for, but freedom isn't free. If you're not sure you have the free time to do what it takes to maintain your freedom by truly vetting your elected leaders now, consider that after your freedom goes away, you'll have even less time for yourself while under the thumb of your unelected leaders later.

## Immigration

Simply ask them this question: Are we a nation of immigrants or citizens? Then sit back and watch the show. You'll learn right away if they're a tool of the corporatist progressive cheap labor industrial complex.

And don't fall for canards on this issue like "we can't deport all these people." Of course we can't, and very few are calling for something that dramatic. Simply deport immediately and permanently any illegals who have committed further crimes while here, offer those with legitimate employment work permits, punitively punish American companies that hire illegals, and then prohibit illegals from access to any government welfare benefits except when human life is immediately at stake.

Those four changes alone would all but eliminate the illegal immigration problem, and nowhere was it required to break up families or any other fake talking points the amnesty peddlers in the Republican Party spew to justify cheap labor for their chamber of commerce pimps. You cannot afford to lose this argument with these people because of what's at stake with the immigration issue—everything.

For example, California now rivals only Washington, DC, as the chief exporter of progressive neo-Marxism to the rest of the country. But it wasn't always this way. From 1952 to 1988, California voted Republican in nine of ten presidential elections. If you're a millennial or younger, that probably blows your mind, but it's true. Which begs the question: what changed?

What changed was President Ronald Reagan's 1986 amnesty. It so changed the demographics of California that the state has been reliably Democrat ever since it was fully implemented. Yes, *that* Ronald Reagan.

Democrats now have such hegemony in the state that they face no competition, and so they've turned California into a cauldron for their most statist and anti-liberty schemes. In fact, the last three GOP presidential nominees didn't even get 40 percent of the vote statewide.

Amnesties are nothing more than Democratic Party new voter drives. They're not compassionate. They're not just. They're not humane.

They're a scam.

There are other ways to show fellow human beings of potential dignity and opportunity, as I just laid out, which doesn't risk the rule of law or our way of life. But we don't go down that road because it's not about any of the lofty ideals we're gaslighted with on this issue. It's about cheap labor for the GOP's donor class, and new voters for Democrats—nothing more, nothing less.

And if you do another amnesty, you will do to Texas what was done to California. Turn Texas blue, and Democrats will pretty much have a death grip on the Electoral College from this time forward. Which would imperil every issue you care about as a conservative or libertarian, even if you're sympathetic to amnesty on the immigration issue. Most of those who receive this amnesty will then turn around and vote against gun rights but for Planned Parenthood. They'll vote against limited government but for expansion of the welfare state. They'll do so because of identity politics, and because they come from parts of the world where Marxism has been cloaked in Christianity.

So, yes, it is true a lot of these illegals are people who believe in God and "family values." But since they've been conditioned that government is there to provide for them (the nanny state view) rather than "bring the sword of righteousness against the evildoer" (the biblical view), they will put their family values on the back burner behind their identity politics/big government demands.

No modern-day Republican presidential candidate did more Hispanic voter outreach than George W. Bush, including his vocal support for more blanket amnesties. While it is true he did better than any other GOP presidential candidate with Hispanics, what they don't tell you is that was a measly 40 percent of the Hispanic vote.[2] Since 1980, Republicans have only gotten above 35 percent of the Hispanic vote *twice*.

This was the argument I made to Senator Marco Rubio when he called me on the phone to lobby me to support his "gang of eight" amnesty proposal in 2013. Rubio was taking a ton of justifiable heat from conservatives for going back on his anti-amnesty rhetoric during his 2010 US Senate campaign and was concerned this would hurt his 2016 presidential aspirations.

When I cited some of these statistics to Rubio and asked him what was in it for my law-and-order audience, he told me that if we didn't back legislative amnesty now, President Barack Obama would do an executive amnesty later. Thus, he would be seen as a

Latino emancipator of sorts, and Democrats would start getting 85 to 90 percent of the growing Hispanic vote, like they already do the black vote, for the foreseeable future.

However, I was unpersuaded by his argument and thought his analysis actually reinforced mine. For if this group can be so heavily swayed by identity politics, then *any* amnesty is political poison regardless of its source—as the result of Reagan's 1986 amnesty already proves. Not to mention, despite his heated rhetoric on the immigration issue, Donald Trump actually got more of the Hispanic vote in 2016 than the more genteel Mitt Romney did in 2012.[3]

Amnesty is a loser issue for us. It's both bad policy and bad politics. Another mass amnesty would be a political Jonestown for conservatism. So vet the true worldview of Republicans asking for your vote on this issue. Don't let them off the hook.

\* \* \* \* \*

We come now to the test of your resolve. I must warn you that by going down this road of truly vetting candidates to find out not where they are but who they truly are, you're going to find the vast majority of Republicans running for office are as useful as mammary glands on a bull.

Many of you reading this still don't want to believe that. You still want to be lied to, so you can root for Team GOP over those dastardly Democrats no matter how much of your own soul—let alone your mind—you lose in the process.

Of course, many of those Democrats are every bit as dastardly as you say, but you're really rooting for the Washington Generals—the team that is supposed to lose, that is set up to lose, so they always do. Nevertheless, you're still waving the pom-poms and singing the fight song of a false front operation.

If that's you, do not ask your candidates any of the questions I just suggested, because you'll either have to continue lying to yourself or do something about it afterward. Or you'll try to find some passive-aggressive way of expressing your outrage, without taking a full-fledged stand that leaves you no wiggle room for grabbing your ankles later—when the GOP's siren song "but the Democrats" blares once more.

A dog returns to its own vomit.

# My Favorite Politician Will Save America

**TRUTH BOMB** *It's far more likely we'll have to save America from your favorite politician than it is any politician will save us.*

No.

## LIE #10

# My Favorite Politician Loves Me

**TRUTH BOMB** *You always love them more than they love you. Never forget that.*

It might have been the most important lesson of my career, and it providentially arrived at the perfect time.

It was Iowa Caucus night 2008. The wife and I braved a wintry evening to head out to what we hoped (and expected) would be Mike Huckabee's (and our own) victory celebration—finalizing perhaps the most stunning upset in the event's history.

The former Arkansas governor was polling in the low single digits until a small but dedicated group of hearty activists, and my statewide radio show, decided to go all in for his candidacy. Months later, though heavily outspent, Huckabee was on his way to getting the most votes by a Republican in caucus history at the time (Ted Cruz would later shatter that record in 2016).

I arrived at the Embassy Suites in downtown Des Moines that night like a conquering hero. I had a swagger. I was Denzel Washington in *Training Day*, "King Kong ain't got nothing on me."

It was a packed house as the returns were being finalized, and with the race called early by the networks there were already numerous grateful Huckabee supporters, who lined up to thank me for my (in my mind obviously vital, pivotal, and crucial) role in his victory once we arrived.

Over and over again I heard stuff like "couldn't have done it without you" and "Huckabee owes you big-time." I posed for more pictures than I could count. It was almost like I was the candidate here. People couldn't yet get to Huckabee, so they clearly chose the next best thing—me.

A well-known DC conservative reporter came up to congratulate me for my role in the night's outcome and interview me for his national publication. It seemed like I had arrived, and I hadn't even been on the air locally for two years yet. All that was missing was "One Shining Moment" playing as I cut down the nets.

After a couple of hours of this, Huckabee had finally completed his long-list of post-victory media requests. He was now free to come and talk to those of us who managed to hang around till the very end. There were still a lot of us. Although I had to work in the morning, with the way my ego was getting stroked, they were gonna have to drag me out of there.

I was at the end of the throng because there was a line of people wanting to talk to me all night long. So I watched as Huckabee worked his way down to me slowly but surely. The anticipation of this glorious moment was building. Clearly he was saving the best (me) for last. After all, I had turned my statewide radio show into a Huckabee Super PAC. I found out later that Mitt Romney's people estimated to one national conservative outlet that my show alone was worth millions in opposition research against them.

I lost track of how many times Huckabee had been with me on my show. We had prayed together privately. Our oldest daughter had her picture taken with him several times. I was asked to emcee a New Year's Eve fundraiser for him, and gladly obliged. My wife, Amy, and I even had some private time with Mike and his wife, Janet, beforehand.

I got to talk strategy with his national campaign manager, Ed Rollins, who I must say did a tremendous job of pretending to care what I thought. I couldn't have been more flattered, to tell you the truth. His Iowa Caucus chairman, Bob Vander Plaats, and I got to be good friends during this campaign and spoke regularly.

Hence, there was little doubt in my mind I was getting quite the helmet sticker when Huckabee finally made his way down to me. Who knows? He might even look at me proudly, turn back to the crowd, and pronounce, "This is my son in whom I am well pleased." And even if that's laying it on a little thick, this was still gonna be a moment I would most certainly never forget.

Indeed it was. Just not in the way I'd anticipated.

Finally, Huckabee had worked enough of the room that we made eye contact and he smiled. I straightened while waiting for my close-up, Mr. DeMille. I was doing my best to play it cool on the outside, when on the inside I was bursting with pride—in myself.

Just as Huckabee was about to reach out to me, someone else came and whispered something in his ear. Huckabee nodded, and started looking for the quickest way out. As he was turning to go he turned to me, and in front of my adoring public (and my wife) professed his undying love to me with these momentous words:

*"Thanks for all your help, Scott."*

I froze, as did what was left of the room. They had all heard it, too. And like that Huckabee was gone, off to New Hampshire presumably. Leaving me alone to deal with the gasps, giggles, and guffaws. For that instant I felt so emasculated I'm pretty sure I could feel my sperm count drop.

As the teenagers say today, it was "awkward!" I was shot through the heart, and Huckabee was to blame. He gave love a bad name.

I think the last time I was that humiliated by another male I was wearing a singlet for the Jackson Park Junior High wrestling team. I only won one match that year, as I lived out every painful page of a *Diary of a Wimpy Kid* novel. And that victory only occurred because the opposing school had so many kids out sick they had to forfeit several weight classes, including my own.

So even my one win was pathetic, though not quite as pathetic as the match when I got pinned in just under a minute by another kid who hadn't won a match all year. I wouldn't go so far as to say I was emotionally scarred by such a jarring pubescent humiliation, but to this day I can't really talk about it without my voice cracking and a nervous tick coming on for some reason.

By Huckabee not even getting my name right in a crowded room, I had gone from my anticipated Roy Hobbs hitting the pennant-winning home run in *The Natural* moment to Ralphie after he shoots his eye out in *A Christmas Story.* Instead of "Hail to the Victors" playing in my head, my ego was serenaded with "What a Fool Believes" by the Doobie Brothers. Speaking of doobies, I could've used one right about then.

But a funny thing happened as I glanced around the room, and my mind began to scheme a way to salvage whatever shred of dignity I had left. I heard that still, small voice in the back of my brain whisper ever so softly, "Don't take yourself too seriously, kid." And right at that very moment, I took its advice.

I laughed at myself—hard.

I laughed at myself, and the ridiculousness of my ego, so hard I almost peed my pants. Heck, I may have even farted out the other end. Then my wife laughed, too, as did several others. Amy and I laughed all the way out to the car in the cold.

Once we got in and turned on the ignition, I turned to her and said, "God taught me a very valuable lesson here tonight. No matter where this radio thing goes from here, I'm just a kid born to a fifteen-year-old mom. I'm here because He has permitted it, and I won't be here a day earlier or a day later than He ordains."

Before we go any further, let me say this right now: none of this was Huckabee's fault. He was merely trying to win an election, which required staying on task. In the following years, he and I would have many more conversations, including interviews on his television program when he totally remembered my first name is Steve. This was exclusively my own fault. While soaking up the adulation of his supporters that evening, I believed I'd won Huckabee's affection.

The issue isn't so much that I thought I had won his affection; it's that I even tried.

I know of no other business where the employers behave this way around their employees. I mean could you imagine if you were a driver or even a regional manager for a national company like UPS and your CEO called you up out of the blue and this is what he said: "Hey, if you're not too busy, could you give me the time of day? Oh, and my kids are asking if they can get a picture with you. Again, if you're not too busy."

You'd think you're either being punked or he's had a nervous breakdown. Because in that business model, no one needs reminding about the order of things. But in our political business model we are all too often fanboys and fangirls. So the order of things is out of whack and reversed, which is causing us to enable our very undoing.

*Corporately as a people we no longer hold our politicians accountable. Instead, we hold in contempt those individuals who are still attempting to do so.*

Case in point, please permit me to share a sample of a conversation I've tragically had all too often throughout my career with people claiming to be conservatives:

**Me:** [Fill in the blank Republican] just voted to [fund Planned Parenthood, raise taxes, grow government, pass amnesty, or pick your poison].

**Too many of you:** Why are you so divisive? What about the Democrats?

**Me:** What do the Democrats have to do with this?

**Too many of you:** Why don't you focus on the Democrats?

**Me:** What do the Democrats have to do with why this Republican just behaved like a Democrat?

**Too many of you:** Why don't you focus on beating Democrats?

**Me:** What's the point of beating Democrats with Republicans who will just behave like them in office?

**Too many of you:** You're helping the Democrats.

**Me:** Um, wouldn't the Republican who actually voted for what Democrats believe be the one helping the Democrats?

**Too many of you:** You're not a real conservative.

**Me:** I'm the one actually standing for conservatism here.

**Too many of you:** Why are you working against us? Why won't you help us win? We have to beat the Democrats.

**Me:** I agree; we have to beat the Democrats, which is why I'm trying to stop the Republicans from just doing what Democrats would do anyway if they could.

**Too many of you:** You're a liberal in disguise and a phony.

**Me:** What have I said that is untrue?

**Too many of you:** You're being divisive and you're hurting us.

**Me:** It doesn't matter what the result of what I'm saying is. What matters is whether or not it's true. So what have I said that is untrue?

**Too many of you (now totally disregarding the information I gave you):** Well, [sellout Republican] is still better than [whatever Democrat we're supposed to hate the most at that time], big tent, and stop being such a theocratic purist (maybe even followed by something vulgar).

**Me:** Sigh.

\* \* \* \* \*

I've had a variation of this conversation so often it has taken years off my life—as well as inches from my hairline, while adding inches onto my waistline from the resulting stress eating. At different times in my career, I've either wanted to hug or slug such people. I thought I was getting into this business to defend the values of these folks. Turns out I had to defend our values from them. For too many of us really only have one thing we value when it's all said and done: Team GOP.

If you bristled at that, or that offended you, I want you to know I am most definitely talking about you. As we say on my show, "When you throw a rock into a pack of dogs, the one that yelps is the one you hit." People like you are absolutely killing us even more than the Left, because you're the reason the Left wins regardless of the election outcome.

Your fanboy/fangirl myopia makes you human shields for douchtastic Republicans, who are better at incrementally implementing progressivism than even the progressives are. Like we would all oppose the largest welfare state program in American history at the time if a Democrat proposed it.[1]

But if it comes from Republican George W. Bush, it's suddenly rebranded "compassionate conservatism" and "you're helping the anti-American Left" if you won't stand and applaud as he fulfills the Left's nocturnal emissions.

In the past few years, we have surrendered all of our moral high ground as a movement. We now no longer hold the line on public policy, personal character, media bias, or anything else we once thought made us better than the godless, heathen Left. Furthermore, we're not even ashamed of it. And if you're not willing to lose your soul for a political party and politicians that have proven time, and time, and time again they're not worth it, then you're accused of "helping the Democrats." By people that are helping the Republicans actually help the Democrats, of course.

I'm tempted to just let you pathetic Gollums have your precious and move on with the rest of my life. But I won't for two reasons:

1. I can't just stand idly by and let you ruin my kids' future unchallenged, just so you can get your groupie on for a political party that sells you out faster than you can say "what about...?"

**2.** I just enjoy breaking my foot off in the backsides of you feckless fools too dang much. So come get your whuppin'.

See, there's the *right* reason I'm gonna kick you Republican dhimmis in the shins with a steel-toed boot to the last, and then there's the *real* reason.

Even if I didn't have kids, as a natural contrarian I have an aversion to cults, so you'd annoy me just as much either way. As long as there's room at the Punk You Inn, I plan on staying awhile.

I did the math, and I figure you Republican dhimmis have taken up so much of my time that you owe me. And I intend to collect. Boy, do I intend to collect. In fact, feel free to consider this book your first installment.

Half-kidding aside, I'm also hoping that directly confronting you in a way that would make Saint Paul dropping bombs on sorcerers in Paphos proud might wake at least some of you up before it's too late and the Constitution is lost to history for good. Just as Huckabee's unintentional public slight once did for me. Publicly flogging me to awaken me from an ego trip to nowhere.

But if not, I suppose I'll just have to settle for a high body count. We all have our crosses to bear. As one of my radio mentors taught me many years ago, if at first you don't succeed, lower your standards.

I guess what I'm trying to say with some subtlety is that if you're part of the problem, please don't get out of the way. Rather, stay right where you are so that we can run over you on the way to the solution.

Now, if you're as frustrated by these Republican dhimmis as I am, but think I'm being a little too harsh here, I'd urge you to reconsider that notion. I'd urge you to follow in my footsteps. And no, the provocative posture I'm proposing isn't unbiblical. Quite the contrary, it follows biblical precedent. For everything there is a time and a season.

There's a time for mercy to triumph over judgment, and then there's a time for swinging the jawbone of an ass. There's a time to rebuild the walls, and then there's a time to tear down the temple to the demon Dagon, plunging his ugly mug face down in the dirt as you do. Can you guess what time it is now?

The future of the greatest civilization east of Eden is at stake, and we ain't got time for you to bat your eyelashes and get the vapors over slimy, gutless politicians who hate you and laugh at you behind your back anyway. We the people are supposed to run the show around here, but we won't until we start acting like we're capable of it.

And it starts by reasserting our supremacy in our relationship with our politicians. They're not our bosses. They're our public servants, and we are their masters. And as Christ said, "No servant is greater than his master."

Do not fawn. Do not fanboy/fangirl. Don't become a groupie. Don't turn them into your celebrity crush on the cover of *Tiger Beat*. Be a freaking adult before your kids grow up, that option is no longer available to them, and they're permanent wards of the welfare state instead.

In our form of government, our politicians cannot take power from us we don't voluntarily surrender (passively or actively) to them. So if they're too powerful, too corrupt, and too unaccountable we have no one to blame but ourselves. For none of them got where they are without us voting them into office.

A well-known and very successful Republican politician, a household name, once responded this way when I asked him why he didn't advocate devolving power from Washington back to state and local governments closer to the people:

*"Do you think the people are really willing, let alone able, to truly govern themselves?"*

Well, do you?

# The Battle is Between
# Conservatives and Liberals

**TRUTH BOMB** *There really aren't any liberals anymore. The battle is really leftists versus what's left of America.*

P ro tip: You're unlikely to win a battle when you don't really know who, or what, you're really battling.

Much of what we call conservatism these days operates under tactical paradigms that are obsolete, and those who don't have unfortunately and incorrectly decided becoming like the very people we're trying to defeat is the way to go. I already addressed that latter group in the previous chapter. Now it's time to address those of you holding on to your virtue, but also a play-book that still parties like it's 1999.

That playbook goes something like this.

About 40 percent of Americans are liberals, and about 40 percent of Americans are conservatives. And elections are won by winning over a majority of those squishy independent folks in the middle. Otherwise known as the great unwashed, swing voters, or fiscal conservatives who are social liberals—so offer them tax cuts with a sprinkling of Sodom and Gomorrah because they love that.

For decades this has been the conventional wisdom of what we call "the GOP smart set," and they believe it is gospel.

Except as Luke Skywalker said to the villainous Kylo Ren in *The Last Jedi*, when he, too, confidently spouted his preferred yet nonsensical narrative: "Amazing—every word of what you just said is wrong."

First of all, the math is now inverted. Over 40 percent of Americans now identify as independents,[1] so right away this playbook is conditioned to reach an audience that has substantially increased since it was first implemented. And if the number of independents is soaring, at the same time the country is becoming more politically polarized than at any point since the lead-up to the Civil War, that's not because more people are walking down the middle of the road unable to choose a side.

It's because they don't want to.

Most people hate the two-party duopoly, while at the same time they're becoming more partisan. If you're operating under the GOP smart set's dilapidated playbook, that doesn't make sense and seems like a contradiction. However, if you're willing to see things as they really are in the here and now, it absolutely makes perfect sense.

*These days, partisanship isn't driven by party affiliation as much as a competing sense of values.*

Yes, tribalism is all the rage these days between declared Republicans and Democrats, as we've discussed aplenty in this book, but each side justifies its tribalism because of their warring and irreconcilable values. So the fear of "the other" drives folks to put up with anything their side does, because the values of "the other" are perceived to be so much worse.

# LIE #11

This sense that there's two Americas, each with a distinctly different set of values, yet attempting to fly the same flag, even permeates today's independents. Yesteryear's independents avoided cultural clashes and existential issues like the plague, just as the GOP smart set says. But that was then, and this is now.

Back then we were merely debating civil unions. Now we're demanding you "bake the cake, bigot."

Back then we were merely debating whether to keep abortion "safe, legal, but rare." Now we're watching videos of dead baby parts being peddled like watches by a sidewalk merchant, as a Planned Parenthood employee with a seared conscience chomps on her Caesar salad.

Back then we were merely debating temporary amnesty for a few million hardworking illegal aliens looking to escape a squalor most Americans blessedly can't even begin to contemplate. Now they're undocumented immigrants, there are many millions more, and you're a xenophobe if you won't voluntarily give up your job for them.

Back then we were merely debating whether former Democratic Party operatives, like the late Tim Russert, should be anchors of major mainstream media programming. Now we're lamenting we don't have fair journalists like Russert anymore.

Back then we were merely concerned the advent of political correctness would turn our college campuses into places where liberal ideology would have an advantage in reaching the next generation. Now, without increasingly rare wins in court, free speech is all but gone from many of America's universities. And popular conservative personalities like Ben Shapiro and Steven Crowder are banned because they may trigger so many snowflakes they'll create campus unrest or something.

Back then we were mostly united that the Soviet Union was the bad guy, and Bernie Sanders was panned for celebrating his honeymoon in Moscow during the Cold War.[2] Now we're injecting defeated Marxist ideology into our bloodstream, and all the cool kids want Sanders to be president.

Back then the late, great Billy Graham was welcome to bring the good news to the White House regardless of which party resided there. Now Democrats like Bill Clinton and Barack Obama, and Republicans like George W. Bush, host Islamic iftar dinners in the White House.

Back then we were incredulous that Murphy Brown believed she didn't need a man around to help her raise her child. Now we think men have a uterus.

All this has happened because a major evolution has taken place within the American Left in our time. Yesterday's liberals are all but gone now. They have been replaced by today's leftists, or driven to the Republican Party because of how far left the Democrats have gone. Which, in turn, has caused the GOP to move left as well, since the definition of "big tent" has taken on a whole new meaning than it once held.

To accommodate these former liberals not willing to become leftists, "big tent" in the GOP has expanded from setting aside specific issue differences to setting aside systemic worldview differences. As a result, the GOP isn't a "big tent" nowadays as much as it's a "big tarp," as in a shelter for people of various and perhaps not reconcilable persuasions, seeking sanctuary from what's effectively become the Communist Party USA. This also explains why the Republicans are so good as a minority party and so terrible as a governing one.

Since conservatism is no longer what holds the party together but fear/opposition to the leftist radicalization of the Democrats, the GOP is great at saying no when it doesn't have to say yes. But then once it successfully beats back the pagan hordes of the Democrats at the ballot box and has to govern, the center cannot hold.

See, a tent has stakes holding up its structure at every corner to prevent its implosion. However, a tarp is simply a covering that can flap in the wind, or even be blown away if the storm is strong enough since there's nothing undergirding it.

With no core worldview uniting it, the GOP simply cannot govern once given power. It has too many vested and ideological interests tugging at it simultaneously, and without the foil and fear of the Democrats to hold it together it splinters. It's not a closed circle but a Venn diagram.

This has all happened to the Republican Party because of the evolution of the Democratic Party from a liberal to a leftist one. Elections are no longer Republicans vs. Democrats, or even conservatives vs. liberals. They've really become what's left of America voting Republican in order to stave off the leftist Democrats.

Here's the real difference between yesterday's liberals and today's leftists: *Yesterday's liberals wanted government to permit you to do stupid or immoral things. Today's leftists want government to command you to do them, and then punish you if you won't.*

Here's what that looks like in our culture:

- ▶ Yesterday's liberals believed in multicultural diversity. Today's leftists believe in statist conformity.
- ▶ Yesterday's liberals were suspicious of authoritarianism. Today's leftists seek to wield it.

- Yesterday's liberals believed in freedom of speech so much they fought to protect even obscenity. Today's leftists find it obscene that you challenge their views and want you to no longer be protected to do so.
- Yesterday's liberals wanted all the kids to read books like *Catcher in the Rye* that encouraged or inspired contrarian thinking/behavior. Today's leftists don't want you reading that because that may encourage or inspire you to have views contrary to theirs.
- Yesterday's liberals believed in softening societal norms. Today's leftists believe in replacing them altogether.
- Yesterday's liberals viewed themselves as champions of dissent. Today's leftists vow you will be made to care if you dare to dissent.
- Yesterday's liberals believed in global cooling.[3] Today's leftists believe in global warming, and if you don't celebrate a holiday started by a dude who murdered and composted his girlfriend[4] you're a "science-denier."
- Yesterday's liberals rallied to political dissidents in totalitarian countries. Today's leftists create dissidents by throwing the likes of Kim Davis[5] in jail, and bankrupting families like the Kleins like any good totalitarian would.[6]

What was once a pro-immigration party is now an open borders one.

What was once a pro-middle-class party now takes jobs away from the middle class because of what the temperature might be ten thousand years from now.

What was once a "government should do for people what they can't do for themselves" party is now a "government should tell you what you can and cannot do" party.

What was once a religiously pluralistic party is now an irreligious one.

What was once a left-of-center political party is now a neo-Marxist one.

How did this happen to the Democratic Party? It was invaded and became infested with the cult of progressivism. You should know I'm using the word "cult" for a very specific reason and not just for dramatic effect.

Progressivism as a movement has all the trappings of being a vehicle for the spirit of the age. It is determined to either distort or deconstruct spiritual orthodoxy and acknowledged morality just as any other cult seeks to do. See, we think of progressivism as simply a rival political ideology—except it's so much more than that, and until we realize that, we cannot defeat it.

Progressivism is a cult driven by a heresy (defined as false and destructive religious teaching), as is every other cult. It seeks to replace the Judeo-Christian religious/moral view that inspired American exceptionalism with a new moral order. To realize this goal, it must replace God with government and the church with state.

Progressivism possesses the same characteristics of any other cult:

> ▶ **A creation story to replace the Biblical account**—In the case of progressivism this is Darwinian evolution, a random and meaningless origin story with no divine accountability. This is why progressives in education always ruthlessly remove any skeptics of Darwin within the faculty. Just as the rest of the Bible falls apart if it's not true that God created the world, so does progressivism collapse if it's true that He did.

▶ **Tools of distortion**—This is the role postmodernism plays for progressivism. It's a contagion unleashed by progressives to take us all the way back to the first lie in the Garden of Eden: "Did God really say?" The point of this exercise is to replace clarity with confusion, and intellectually give people who succumb to it permission to be their own gods by determining what's true for them. Once a culture accepts there is no absolute truth (which, in and of itself, is an absolute but they conveniently sidestep that fact), it will then start standing for "my truth." And if you disagree with someone's personal truth, or point out to them it's total manure, you're a bigot, of course.

▶ **Promotion of moral insanity**—Cults either ignore the restraints God puts on human behavior for our own good or demand some unattainable super-morality of people beyond what God requires in order to impose compliance to the cult at all costs. In the case of progressivism, it's actually doing both. On one hand, progressivism in our day has successfully removed most of the moral restraints previous generations acknowledged to their benefit. And now we are actively aiding and abetting our own self-destruction if you look at the fallout (surge in fatherlessness, STDs, and so on.) from the sexual revolution as just one example. At the same time, progressivism is demanding we find some way of communicating what we believe that never offends those who don't share our beliefs. That's simply not an attainable goal, which is precisely progressivism's point. If you can't share what you believe when it's contrary to progressivism without offending a progressive, then you lose your right to espouse your beliefs at all.

▶ **Individual worth replaced with group-think**—Since
a Judeo-Christian worldview begins with the premise
that each of us is created individually in the image of
God, it places a high emphasis on the rights and pur-
suits of happiness of the individual. However, cults
always coerce individuals into giving up their individual
identity in order to comply with the collective. This is
known as "group-think," and it's the force that binds
the progressive galaxy together. For once a person
ceases to see themselves as part of a collective and as an
actual person, they are much more likely to abandon
the identity politics that is progressivism's intellectual
compound. On the other hand, as long as a person is
immersed in identity politics, they will conform to the
group-think even to their own detriment. For example,
black unemployment in America hit a record low in
May of 2018.[7] But when hip-hop superstar Kanye West
started challenging progressivism's cultish dogma right
around that time, he was called "a gift to racists"[8] by a
white progressive in the mainstream media. If you dare
think for yourself, a cult will turn on you every time.
The same thing happened to another black hip-hop
artist, Ginuwine, when he refused to kiss a dude who
pretends to be a chick on national television. Since
gender dysphoria ranks higher on the intersectional-
ity ranking of victim classes than simply being black,
Black Entertainment Television said Ginuwine's refusal
to violate his conscience put "the Internet at war."[9]
Ginuwine's cardinal sin was believing he could put his
individual values ahead of the group-think's demands.

▶ **Suffering for those on the inside, and persecution for those who challenge it from the outside**—Except for its privileged leaders, everyone else in a cult suffers by belonging to it. Progressives have run Chicago for eighty-seven years, Baltimore for fifty-one years, and Houston for thirty-seven years. Those three cities by themselves *combined for almost half of the nationwide rise in the murder rate between 2014 and 2016.*[10] In other words, decades of slavishly voting for progressivism has literally gotten people in those cities killed. And that's not even counting all of the aborted babies. If you dare challenge the cult's stranglehold on its people from the outside, then you will face persecution. Whether you be a Christian baker or florist who refuses to serve a homosexual union contrary to your morality. Whether you're a conservative or religious group on campus at a public university that advocates for any form of traditionalism. Whether you're a minority who breaks the bondage of identity politics and is now branded a traitor for preferring to be acknowledged for your individual achievements instead. Oh, and neutrality isn't an option to the cult. You either affirm it or you are its enemy. Peaceful coexistence simply doesn't exist. So you will join the cult, or you will be made to care.

The cult of progressivism has taken over the Democratic Party, and the result is its transition from a liberal political party to a leftist one. This leftist evolution of the Democratic Party has created a crack in America's foundation, and it's grown to the point of launching an existential crisis that threatens the future of the country. Or at least the country we were originally founded to be. It's a crack poised to become a fissure. And a fissure eventually becomes a schism.

This crack in America's foundation is felt by all—including independents.

Prior to the 2016 election the *Washington Post* did a fascinating study called "The Myth of the Independent Voter."[11] What they found is, unlike in previous eras, many of today's independents absolutely know where they stand on the issues. They're just not sure either political party does.

That's especially true if you're what they called a "Republican-leaning independent" in their analysis. These are voters who aren't interested in being identified with the Republican Party because they don't believe it's sincere or they don't want to be associated with its brand. Yet come Election Day, they usually come home to vote GOP in order to try and stop the values Democrats stand for.

On the other hand, "Democrat-leaning independents" fell into two categories: in favor of Democrats' big government programs but not their social agenda (i.e., the types of voters Trump converted in 2016), or voters who aren't sure Democrats are going left enough fast enough.

*Translation: today's independent voters are more ideologically partisan, but not as politically partisan.*

Most of the GOP consultant industry is at best outdated, and a brood of vipers at worst, because they have more ideologically in common with Democrats than they do with us. So they're not even trying to win a battle they don't believe in, which is why they aren't even bringing knives to a gunfight. It's more like bringing sporks to the O.K. Corral. One side has their phasers set to kill.

The other side doesn't even have phasers, but hopes to negotiate a settlement with an enemy who doesn't take hostages.

This is now where some of you will say something like, "But Steve, this is exactly why we have to fight dirty like they do."

Borrowing their tactics will not elevate our cause but undermine it, because you can't claim to be for morals, standards, truth, and the rule of law when you're behaving like those who do not. And since we probably squeezed the last bit of Miracle Whip from the bottle of "silent majority" in 2016, we're facing an emerging generation that knows more about gender fluidity than they do the Holocaust.[12] Not to mention their men are just as likely to still be living at home with mom as they are married with children.

So we better figure out pretty quickly how to evangelize to a new generation that never knew Bruce Jenner as the ultimate portrayal of vigorous masculinity by winning the Olympic decathlon. They think he's a she.

If we model the soulless Saul Alinsky playbook to them, they will recognize it because it's what they were indoctrinated into already (see David Hogg). Thus, they will also recognize that's not us, that we're counterfeit frauds. They'll call us hypocrites (which is a mortal sin to millennials) and just go with the real thing instead.

Lies cannot defeat liars. Shilling cannot defeat shills. Tribalists cannot defeat tribalism. Right-wing media propaganda cannot defeat left-wing media bias. Clickservatism will not advance conservatism.

Leftists have victoriously completed what influential Marxist thinker and strategist Antonio Gramsci called "the long march through the institutions."[13] They control every influential sector of secular society now and are advancing upon the sacred as we speak, with Pope Francis sounding more like Che Guevara than Saint Peter, and the evangelical leaders who haven't clowned themselves for Team GOP sounding more like social justice warriors than the Apostles.

In short, we don't have the numbers to beat them at their own game. And if we try, we will drive the next generation even deeper into their camp. Which means you may well live to see the day Reagan warned us about. The day when we'd have to explain to our children what it was once like in the United States of America, when we were free.

Therefore, we need tactics that add to the credibility of our arguments, rather than tactics that diminish the credibility of our convictions.

*We fight as hard has the Left, but not like the Left.*

So how do we do that? Unfortunately, the answer to that question would take a whole other book to properly answer. Fortunately, I already wrote that book. It's called *Rules for Patriots: How Conservatives Can Win Again*, and it was written specifically to be the tactical antidote to what leftist radicalization is doing to the country—to put us on the offensive and them on the defensive for a change.

With its Ten Commandments of Political Warfare, there's never been a book like it written for our movement, which is why it was endorsed by a who's who of conservative leaders. And that's also why you should go to Amazon.com right now and buy a copy of it.

# Courts Make the Law.
# So Anything Some Leftist Judge
# Conjures Up from the Bowels
# of His Debased Mind
# is Now the Law

**TRUTH BOMB** *Our founding fathers would've tarred and feathered some of these judges by now.*

I'm gonna warn you right away. This will be a long chapter. That's because we'll be discussing what I believe is the most pressing political issue of the day. It's just that most of you reading this unfortunately don't even realize it, because much of what we call "conservatism" refuses to confront it for reasons only Allah knows. But I do know Allah is pleased this is the case.

What we'll be discussing in this chapter is the Left's weapon of mass destruction, which it has used to almost extinguish American exceptionalism altogether. The Left decrees policies via fiat that would've likely had a very difficult time making it through the normal legislative process.

But to truly understand how much the Left has laid waste to our constitutional republic through the courts, I invite you to join me in the time machine as we travel back to September 17, 1787.

We arrive at the Constitutional Convention in Philadelphia, just as its delegates are meeting to ratify the United States Constitution they had been working on for four months. You want to give this collection of flawed yet wise men a look into the future at the rule of law they were formally establishing. You tell them you come from over two hundred years in the future, when the United States of America of your time has been recognized as the dominant superpower in the world for almost a century now.

You bring with you articles for them to read. The headlines tell about what is happening to the future nation they are forging this very day. They would be pleased to see America fulfill her "manifest destiny," create opportunity for unprecedented individual wealth, and evolve into a technological marvel.

On the other hand, beneath the surface of all that prosperity they would detect dangerous cracks forming in her foundation. Soul-crushing debt, soulless decadence, subsidized anti-American indoctrination cleverly called "education," pointlessly becoming the world's police force, ejecting God from the public square, bathroom and pronoun wars, a free press in bondage to its biases when it's not sensationalizing the trivial, sieve-like borders, and the size of government growing well beyond the eighteen enumerated powers in the Constitution they are about to ratify.

They would surely be astonished and dismayed to see the nation to which they pledged their lives, fortunes, and sacred honors so easily disregard its birthright—without a shot fired from a foreign armada invading her shores, but because we just don't give a damn anymore.

"What has happened in the future to the will of the people, whom we put in charge, that they would elect representatives capable of such treachery," our founding fathers would most certainly ask.

With a heavy heart, you explain that *much of this wasn't done by the people but to the people.* "What sort of fiend is responsible," they demand to know next.

And that's when you show them the following headlines:

- "Courts Make Baby Killing the Law of the Land."
- "Courts Change Six-Thousand-Year-Old Definition of Marriage."
- "Courts Say You Can't Deport Illegal Aliens."
- "Courts Say Taxpayers Have to Subsidize Illegal Aliens."
- "Courts Say Government Can Take Your Century Farm if It Wants Your Land for a Strip Mall Instead."
- "Courts to Rule On Whether the Second Amendment to the US Constitution Is Still Constitutional."
- "Courts Agree You Have to Buy a Product from a Private Company You Don't Want, Because Government Owns You."
- "Courts Take Prayer Out of the Public Schools, and Any Other Reference to God for That Matter."
- "Courts Tell Christians to 'Bake the Cake, Bigot.' but Pagans Can Deny Service to Christians if They Want."
- "Courts Order Castration Surgeries for All Military Personnel That Suddenly Decide They Feel Pretty."

Upon reading these headlines, these men we now know as our founding fathers would be royally pissed off. And not at the judges/courts who did this to us—but at us for letting them get away with it.

"We locked and loaded at Lexington and Concord over lesser intrusions upon our God-given rights," they would say. "And today we're giving you this Constitution so that you don't have to take up arms against your own government, but rather the people get to *be the government*. But what's the point of all this, and all that we lost fighting for independence, if you're just going to give it away to a bunch of black-robed masters we would've tarred and feathered after even one of these outrages?"

Now let me stop right there, because I'm guessing at least one of you reading this has been so intellectually removed from the founding vision of the country, you think tarring and feathering is a human rights violation. You probably read about it on the website of a "human rights group," which also supports dismembering and murdering helpless babies before they are born for population control or something.

The primary purpose our founding fathers used tarring and feathering was to embarrass and shame egregious acts of chicanery and hackery by government bureaucrats. According to the *Journal of the American Revolution*[1]—whose work has been featured by such noted right-wing entities as the *New York Times* and *Time* magazine (note the sarcasm)—tarring and feathering was a "warning not to arouse the community again. There are *no* examples of people in Revolutionary America dying from being tarred and feathered."

The fact we're offended by the tactics used by the generations responsible for our freedom in the first place tells you all you need to know about how we lost our country to high school water boys that went to a pagan law school. Revolutionary America took on the Redcoats, the most feared fighting force in the world at the time. We won't take on a three-judge panel of asexuals from the 666th District of Babylon.

*The founding fathers risked going too far to be free. We won't really risk anything at all.*

I get it, man, I really do. I mean, you might offend third-cousin Elmer you see for five minutes each Thanksgiving, and if he calls you another name on Facebook it just might break you. Not to mention risking the indignity of PEZDISPENER69ME blowing up your mentions on Twitter. Oh, the humanity!

Maybe, just maybe, if we really knew what it was our founding fathers were fighting for, it would inspire us to fight, too? So put your thinking caps on and pay attention. I'm about to talk to you like you're an actual adult. I'm going to do my best to minimize my trademark snark from here on out, and soberly try and fill you in on the cultural hijacking that has taken place, leading to the loss of our inheritance as Americans. I'm going to show you who did it, and how they went about it.

We're going to cover a lot of ground here, so please pay close attention. Feel free to go back and read this chapter more than once. What you're about to read is a summation of a decade of my work and research on this topic. It was inspired by my being on the front lines of my state's historic judicial retention election back in 2010, when for the first time ever voters removed state supreme court justices from office specifically in protest of what they viewed as an unconstitutional decision.

When I'm done here, if I do this right, you're probably going to be angry at some of my peers in our industry for keeping this from you.

Good.

Some of the same men gathered in Philadelphia to ratify our Constitution that day were also there on July 4, 1776—the day the Declaration of Independence was ratified by the Continental Congress.

Otherwise known as the organic law (or source of law) of this nation, the Declaration of Independence asserts what was a radical premise at the time, and in elite sectors of media, academia, and government in our day still is:

> We hold these truths to be self-evident, that all men are created equal, that they are endowed by their Creator with certain unalienable (or God-given) Rights, that among these are Life, Liberty and the pursuit of Happiness. That to secure these rights, Governments are instituted among Men, deriving their just powers from the consent of the governed.

In a nutshell, these are "the Laws of Nature and Nature's God" that Thomas Jefferson, its author, is referring to in its opening paragraph. He reminds us that men are created, or in other words that they are made by God. He asserts that their Creator (God) is alone the granter of rights fundamental to human existence, and names several of the rights God has granted to us such as life, liberty, and the pursuit of happiness. Jefferson punctuates this premise by saying it's so obvious it's self-evident, restating the truth of Psalm 14:1: "The fool says in his heart there is no God."

Jefferson goes on to remind us that governments are established to secure these God-given rights. Since God is "not a respecter of persons" (meaning everyone is equal in the sight of God, regardless of gender, race, station, socioeconomic status, and so on), power ultimately flows from the people to the ruling class as opposed to the other way around (i.e., "government by the consent of the governed").

To justify breaking away from the British Crown, which was a controversial notion to certain aspects of Christian thought at the time, who believed *any* rebellion against earthly authority amounted to rebellion against the God who permitted it, Jefferson lists a series of "repeated injuries and usurpations" committed by the Crown, leading to what he described as "the establishment of an absolute Tyranny." The word "absolute" is key here.

Jefferson is making the case that it is not the colonists who are disobeying God but King George III, who has declared himself "absolute" sovereign in all their affairs, including those God says to render unto Him alone. Therefore, since King George III is effectively declaring himself to be a god, it is the colonists who are obeying the true God by revolting against the king.

They are not radicals but rather disciples. Following in the footsteps of the Apostles, who in the face of persecution for their faith still vowed to "obey God and not man." And then most of them were martyred for refusing to comply with government's demands to worship the state as god rather than the one, true God.

Much of what I just told you has been scrubbed from your history books and I'm guessing is new information to many of you, despite the fact the intended audience for this book is primarily conservatives. In other words, we're attempting to conserve a legacy we don't even know. So if conservatives by and large don't know this stuff, how much of it do you think the public at large knows?

Which is why the prophet of old once said, "My people perish for lack of knowledge" (of their birthright, heritage, intended purpose, and so forth).

Many Americans today believe the tyranny that primarily angered our founding fathers was "taxation without representation." While that was certainly one of their battle cries, that particular usurpation is only listed once by Jefferson. However, several other times Jefferson refers to specific problems with the judiciary on his list. Those problems represented the erosion of the rule of law to our founding fathers.

Here's how our founding fathers restored the rule of law via the Constitution.

They used half of the Bill of Rights (amendments four through eight) to clearly define the legal rights of every US citizen. They established a separation of powers, with three branches of government whose jurisdictions are clearly defined in the Constitution. Unlike the British Crown's system, which had the judiciary serving as a subsidiary of the executive branch (in this case the king), our judiciary would be given independence to provide a true system of checks and balances between the three branches.

However, it is interesting to note that the Constitution provides very limited means for the judiciary to place that check on the other two branches. It's given the fewest enumerated powers (three) of the three branches. The legislative branch is given the means to limit the jurisdiction of the judicial branch, and the judiciary is the only branch whose resources on the federal level (funding and appointments) are completely at the mercy of the other two branches.

It's obvious by these actions that while our Founders felt their legal rights were usurped by a British judicial system serving at the mercy of a tyrannical monarch, as opposed to acting independently in the best interests of its constituents, they were equally wary of replacing a monarchy with an oligarchy. As a result, they made that independent judiciary the weakest of the three branches in order to avoid having the people ultimately ruled by judges they did not elect—which goes against their creed of "government by the consent of the governed."

*The Federalist Papers* were distributed nationwide by several framers of the Constitution at the time of its ratification to explain why they did what they did. *Federalist 78* was written by Alexander Hamilton as a response to those known as anti-Federalists. The Anti-Federalists were concerned that even a judicial branch with only three enumerated powers would still have the means to acquire much more in the future, with judges insulated from the scrutiny of voters via lifetime appointments.

To soothe these justifiable fears, which have proven true in our time, Hamilton wrote that the judiciary is "beyond comparison the weakest of three branches":

The judiciary, on the contrary, has no influence over either the sword or the purse; no direction either of the strength or of the wealth of the society; and can take no active resolution whatever. It may truly be said to have neither *force* nor *will*, but merely judgment; and must ultimately depend upon the aid of the executive arm even for the efficacy of its judgments.

Unfortunately, what Hamilton is describing here sounds precisely nothing like the judicial branch that rules over us today.

When I was a kid, in between Saturday morning cartoons like *Thundarr the Barbarian* we used to watch animated shorts called *Schoolhouse Rock!* One of my favorites was called "I'm Just a Bill (on Capitol Hill)."[2] It described the process for making laws in America. Strangely enough, it never said a word about courts/

judges making laws, and only talked about the executive and legislative branches.

We still refer to legislators, and not judges, as "lawmakers." But let's not kid ourselves: the unelected judges, not the legislators you elect, are usually the ones making the law (or at least what we treat as the law) around here.

Supreme Court Justice Sonia Sotomayor admitted this when she said, "All of the legal defense funds out there are looking for people with court of appeals experience, because court of appeals is where policy is made."[3]

Our founding fathers would smack us for letting this come true.

How did we get here? How did we drift so far from what our founders intended? When did we decide it didn't matter what millions of registered voters think on Election Day nearly as much as what one judge or a small panel of judges thinks? And no matter how stinkin' their thinkin' may be, we must comply or else? Even if it explicitly contradicts the actual wording of the Constitution? Even if it means directly disobeying the God who grants us our rights?

Those are good questions. Now let me ask some even better ones:

- ▶ What is the law?
- ▶ Where does the law ultimately come from?
- ▶ What should we base our laws on?
- ▶ Are some laws higher than others?
- ▶ If some laws are higher than others, how do we know which laws are the higher ones?
- ▶ Who decides such things?

Have you ever heard such questions discussed or debated in conservative movement/media circles? Such a shame you haven't, because apart from the spiritual condition of the people, questions such as these are the most crucial assessment for determining the existential fate of any human civilization. But hey, dude, we'll get right on it after we binge respond to some has-been airhead from Hollyweird on Twitter. Gots to get dem clicks, yo!

Thus once more let me teach you what you don't know, which isn't your fault. You can't know what you were never taught.

It all started in the later nineteenth century, when humanists heavily inspired by Marxist social theory and Darwinian ethics (see *The Descent of Man*) began their takeover of the nation's elite universities. This included Harvard, which was one of the primary targets because it served as the feeder school for most of America's law schools.

Gone was Sir William Blackstone and his *Commentaries on the Laws of England*, which was hugely influential in shaping the legal minds of many of our founding fathers. Unfortunately for Blackstone, he was now on the "wrong side of history" for writing stuff like "law as order of the universe":

> Thus when the Supreme Being formed the universe, and created matter out of nothing, He impressed certain principles upon that matter, from which it can never depart, and without which it would cease to be. When He put the matter into motion, He established certain laws of motion, to which all movable bodies must conform. And, to descend from the greatest operations to the smallest, when a workman forms a clock, or other piece of mechanism, he establishes at his own pleasure certain arbitrary laws for its direction; as that the

hand shall describe a given space in a given time; to which law as long as the work conforms, so long it continues in perfection, and answers the end of its formation. If we further advance, from mere inactive matter to vegetable and animal life, we shall find them still invariable. The whole progress of plants, from the seed to the root, and from thence to the seed again; the method of animal nutrition, digestion, secretion and all the branches of vital economy; are not left to chance, or the will of the creature itself, but are performed in a wondrous involuntary manner, and guided by unerring rules laid down by the great Creator.[4]

What you just read is what Jefferson meant by the "Laws of Nature and Nature's God" in the Declaration of Independence. This is why Jefferson used the term "unalienable." It means preexistent, nontransferable, and therefore incapable of being taken away. In other words, since God alone grants us our rights, no government is empowered to take them away.

Furthermore, since God alone is the author of creation and has revealed His character through it, human beings made in His image have a responsibility to as best they can align their laws with His character. Especially since He has embedded within the creation self-enforcing penalties for repeat or serious violations of His will. Sort of like why a parent scolds a child for touching a hot stove—they don't want that which they created in love to get burned.

This legal theory is what we call "natural law," and adherence to it helped give birth to the greatest nation in the history of creation. It even inspired a system that permitted us the power to correct our own injustices, and for new generations to right the wrongs of previous ones.

149

But when you're out to prove "ye be like God" this just won't do. So Blackstone was out, and Thomas Malthus was now in.

In his autobiography, Darwin credited Malthus as his spirit animal, inspiring Darwin to reduce mankind to a randomly evolved animal with cognitive ability, with no greater purpose than to exist for the purpose of existing and serving the ecosystem:

> In October 1838, that is, fifteen months after I had begun my systematic inquiry, I happened to read for amusement Malthus on *Population*, and being well prepared to appreciate the struggle for existence which everywhere goes on from long-continued observation of the habits of animals and plants, it at once struck that under these circumstances favorable variations would tend to be preserved, and unfavorable ones to be destroyed. The results of this would be the formation of a new species. Here, then I had at last got a theory by which to work.[5]

Sounding like the galactic villain Thanos in *Avengers: Infinity War*, who sees himself as a savior by committing genocide upon people he's convinced the universe is incapable of feeding, Malthus believed in what he called "positive and preventative checks" to save us from the very dystopian future his remedies would ironically usher in.[6]

According to Malthus, the "positive checks" were "higher mortality caused by famine, disease, and war necessary to bring the number of people back in line with the capacity to feed them." Malthus's "preventative checks" included some things that conservatives might agree on, such as moral restraint and abstinence. However, should those fail Malthus also believed in regulating the population of the lesser classes, of course, since they were more likely to be a drain on the system.

Darwin proved Malthus as his inspiration with this quote from his *Descent of Man:* "The Western nations of Europe...now so immeasurably surpass their former savage progenitors [that they] stand at the summit of civilization...The civilized races of man will almost certainly exterminate and replace the savage [non-European or white] races throughout the world."[7]

And those quotes are not a one-off from Darwin's work, which is replete with white supremacy and racist rantings. As Malthus inspired Darwin, so did Darwin inspire Margaret Sanger, the founder of Planned Parenthood and perhaps the most influential woman of the twentieth century.

Here's a sampling of Sanger's greatest hits:[8]

- ▶ She proposed a "parliament of population" that would decide who should be born or allowed to immigrate to the country based on "taste, fitness, and interest of the individuals."
- ▶ She called killing children in the womb "defending the unborn against their disabilities."
- ▶ Sanger believed our immigration policies should "keep the doors of immigration closed to the entrance of certain aliens whose condition is known to be detrimental to the stamina of the race, such as feebleminded, idiots, morons, insane, syphilitic, epileptic, criminal, professional prostitutes, and others in this class." Notice she's dividing people not by behavior but by their class and condition.
- ▶ Sanger argued for "a stern and rigid policy of sterilization and segregation to that grade of population whose

progeny is already tainted, or whose inheritance is such that objectionable traits may be transmitted to offspring."

▸ She advocated for what she called "the American Baby Code," which would "protect society against the propagation and increase of the unfit." Of course, those who believed such as her are who gets to determine who is and isn't unfit.

▸ She believed "the most serious evil of our times is that encouraging the bringing into the world large families. The most immoral practice of the day is breeding too many children." So she advocated birth control, not just as a means of population control, but for the "facilitation of the process of weeding out the unfit" (there's that word again).

▸ She hoped these efforts would bring about "a new race." Which wasn't going to include blacks, who she referred to as "human weeds." In a 1939 letter, Sanger wrote "we don't want the word to go out that we want to exterminate the Negro population"[9] in describing her "Negro Project." The goal was to hire "three or four colored ministers, preferably with social-service backgrounds, and with engaging personalities. The most successful educational approach to the Negro is through a religious appeal." That's because "the minister is the man who can straighten out the idea [we're trying to exterminate black people] if it ever occurs to any of their more rebellious members."

Right about now, you're probably thinking, "Golly, Steve, this all sounds more like the KKK than the USA, and more like Hitler than George Washington." Well, if you're thinking that, you're right. And while I find Nazi/Hitler references the stuff of intellectual laziness, when it looks like a duck and quacks like a duck—it's a duck.

After all, Sanger affirmed Nazi eugenics (or junk science for racists) and in 1926 spoke publicly at a KKK rally.[10] If we fast-forward to our time, we see the 2016 Democrat nominee for president of the United States, Hillary Clinton, say the following after receiving an award named after Sanger: "Now, I have to tell you that it was a great privilege when I was told that I would receive this award. I admire Margaret Sanger enormously, her courage, her tenacity, her vision...*I am really in awe of her.*"[11]

A woman who professes her admiration for a racist that detested every Judeo-Christian ideal the country was founded upon won a majority of the popular vote in the 2016 presidential election. It's highly unlikely many of the people who voted for her even knows any of this. Let that sink in for a moment.

Here's what all this means.

In order to implement this New Moral Order, you have to get rid of the old one. And since it's unlikely a people that sings "God Bless America" are going to voluntarily in one fell swoop merge onto the Highway to Hell, you have to gradually lead them there. And while the late Andrew Breitbart's axiom "politics flows downstream from culture" is spot on, before you can infiltrate a culture you have to overturn their rule of law.

For it is the rule of law that protects a people from cultural infiltration. If the rule of law aligns with the "Laws of Nature and Nature's God," so will most of the culture—out of fear of the legal consequences for doing otherwise if nothing else.

But once the rule of law erodes, or is removed altogether, there goes the primary protector of any culture. Then once government goes from punishing evil to endorsing it, you're going to get more evil. Much. More. See my previous book, *A Nefarious Plot.*

This is why the neo-Marxist progressives went after the law long before they had the grip on culture they currently enjoy: *their conquest of the rule of law is what permitted them to grab hold of the culture.*

It's how we go from the Hays Code of yesteryear, which sought to ensure what came out of Hollywood was wholesome and affirmed American values, to nominating a film celebrating the hideous ancient practice of pederasty for best picture nowadays.[12]

When the rule of law changes, a people will respond one of two ways:

1. *They will change with it actively and align their behaviors and desires to what the law now says is acceptable.* You see this with millennials being twice as likely to identify as LGBT as previous generations as just one example.[13]

2. *They will conform to it passively by thinking it's pointless to resist.* And you'll start to say things like, "I don't agree with this, but who am I to impose what I believe on someone else?" All the while they're imposing what you say you don't agree with on you, of course. However, most people don't believe you can fight city hall. So when they see the law change, even if their personal moral compass doesn't, often their resolve to stand up for it will.

Once these barriers are down, the culture is ripe for the taking.

America's law schools are so far gone, a friend of mine who was an appointee in the Reagan administration back in the day once told me, "I took two semesters of constitutional law in law school, and we never once read from or directly quoted the Constitution itself in class. We read lots of people's opinions about what the Constitution supposedly says or means, but never the Constitution itself."

And the reason why is because the Constitution—or the fixed standard, or the natural law, or that which we are to conform to—is irrelevant now. Our opinion of what it says matters more than what it says for itself.

That way we can make it say anything we want it to say, and then once the gavel bangs—presto-chango—that's the new law! So throw off restraint. Ignore all boundaries. Eat, drink, and be merry. For tomorrow liberty dies.

If only our founding fathers could've foreseen this might happen. They might've warned us. They might've put mechanisms in place to save us from judicial oligarchy.

They did.

The man who wrote our national mission statement, Jefferson, was preoccupied with the potential for judicial tyranny. He tried to warn us in the latter years of his public life with words such as these:

> The Constitution, on this hypothesis, is a mere thing of wax in the hands of the judiciary, which they may twist and shape into any form they may please...You seem to consider the judges the ultimate arbiters of all constitutional questions; a very dangerous doctrine indeed, and one which would place us under the despotism of an oligarchy...When the legislative or executive functionaries act unconstitutionally, they are

responsible to the people in their elective capacity. The exemption of the judges from that is quite dangerous enough. I know of no safe depository of the ultimate powers of the society, but the people themselves...But the Chief Justice says, "there must be an ultimate arbiter somewhere." True, there must; but the ultimate arbiter is the people...there is no danger I apprehend so much as the consolidation of our government by the noiseless, and therefore unalarming, instrumentality of the Supreme Court.[14]

As we quoted Hamilton saying earlier in this chapter, to prevent Jefferson's fears from becoming our reality, they made the judicial branch wholly and solely dependent on the other two branches. Its nominees are selected by the executive, and must be confirmed by the legislative. It's funding must be established by the legislative, which means they can remove that funding when the judiciary clearly exceeds its mandate.

In fact, did you know the Constitution even permits the legislative branch to strip the courts of their jurisdiction?

For example, in the George W. Bush years when Republicans had total control of Washington, there was nothing stopping them from passing a law that simply said the following: "Under US Code a 'person' shall be deemed as such from the moment of conception, and therefore afforded all equal protections under the law as prescribed by the Fourteenth Amendment, and there will be no judicial review of this legislation."

Bam—just like that, *Roe v. Wade* is effectively no more.

"Come on, Steve," you'll tell me. "It can't be that simple."

Except it is. But what do I know? I was merely the tip of the spear of the only successful ouster of state supreme court justices over their unconstitutional ruling in American history.[15]

LIE #12

Our founding fathers did not give us a complicated system. They gave us a simple one for ordinary people to hold their government extraordinarily accountable. It has only been made complicated because the devil is always in the details.

Thus, the more we have departed from the clarity of the natural law, the more confusing our laws have become, and the more laws to clarify that confusion we've had to write. And the more laws we pass, the more lost the true law becomes.

Welcome to Babel.

Ironic, isn't it, that the same progressives who bemoan books in the Bible like Leviticus for all their laws are dwarfed in word and scope by the laws the progressives have put on the books. For example, the first five books of the Bible (which include Leviticus), written by Moses, combined are 174,733 words. However, Title 21 of the US Code governing food and drugs is almost seven hundred thousand words all by itself![16]

When progressives bemoan so many laws, what they really mean is they don't like laws that forbid us from doing the things God says not to do. Otherwise, they love laws! They can't get enough laws. We got laws, upon laws, upon laws—as we become more and more lawless.

Our law schools are so tainted by this garbage, the old mantra of "vote Republican to get good judges" is like suing the restaurant that gave you the food poisoning that robbed you of your appetite for your recent weight loss.

All the worst Supreme Court decisions of the last generation—like *Roe v. Wade*, *Kelo v. New London*, *Obergefell v. Hodges*, and more—were decided by Supreme Courts with a majority of Republican appointees. The appointment of John Roberts as a relatively young chief justice was considered the conservative crown jewel of George W. Bush's tenure. And Roberts has turned right around and saved Obamacare—twice!

The first time, Roberts literally rewrote Obamacare's mandate as a tax, even though lawyers for the Obama administration specifically testified before the Supreme Court the mandate wasn't a tax in their view. Yet Roberts magically believed he knew what Obamacare was meant to be more than the people who actually wrote it.

The second time, Roberts changed the meaning of the term "state exchange" to mean a federal exchange. Because, why not? We're already changing the definition of marriage, life, science, reason, and everything else. Knock yourself out.

I could write an entire separate book on all the anti-constitutional decisions made by GOP-appointed judges in lower courts as well. For instance, the judge who threw out the votes of seven million Californians who wanted to protect marriage was a Republican nominee. Heck, even the lawyer arguing to redefine marriage before the US Supreme Court was a Republican appointee. And when Ted Olson was asked on television about his basis for overturning six thousand years of marriage law precedent, he replied, "the Supreme Court never said marriage was between a man and a woman."[17]

So for six thousand years our species didn't know what a marriage was until nine people on the US Supreme Court in 2015 defined it for us? The hubris of these people! I'm not sure the US Supreme Court has ever defined gravity, either. So until they do, keep your feet on the ground and keep reaching for the stars.

Now, I get it—for many of you reading this, the definition of marriage isn't what floats your boat. You still naively think the sexual revolution will permit you to stay morally neutral. Or you're calling yourself a libertarian now, which to you simply means "a conservative that doesn't want to address morality." So let me apply what we've done to the rule of law to an issue that will have unanimous approval among every vestige of conservatism—the Second Amendment.

In 2008, by a slim five to four vote, the US Supreme Court upheld the constitutionality of the Second Amendment in *D.C. v. Heller*. By. One. Vote. Suppose that case had gone five to four the other way? Do we all just turn in our guns the next day? Come on, man, them's the rules, remember? Whenever the judges speak it's like thus speaketh Zarathustra. That's what "conservative media" tells us, right?

When the Supreme Court finally finds the Second Amendment null and void—and mark my words: on our current trajectory, they eventually will—I'm sure you'll all line up at the local federal building to either register your weapons or turn them in.

After all, it's the "settled law" because the judges said so. But don't worry; lots of folks in "conservative media" will write some killer blogs that day about how crappy a deal this is. Then we'll all move on to tomorrow's anti-CNN meme.

No wonder the Left is winning. You'd win, too, if your opponents permitted you to set up a mechanism by which unelected bureaucrats with lifetime appointments get to shove your filth down everyone's throats whenever they darn well please.

So the other two branches of government have lost their manly parts. Our law schools are systemically corrupt to the point even the "conservatives" come out sounding like progressive icon Oliver Wendell Holmes Jr. And the Left just runs to the federal courts to nullify elections whenever they lose. Who or what can save us now?

While behind bars in 1963 for his nonviolent civil rights protests, Martin Luther King Jr. penned his famous *Letter from a Birmingham Jail*. It was a response to a group of white clergymen, who agreed with King about the evils of racial injustice but believed the battle for equality should take place in the courts rather than the public domain. King questions whether a system that for centuries enabled racial inequality can suddenly be trusted to act righteously without external pressure:

> There are just laws and there are unjust laws. I would be the first to advocate obeying just laws. One has not only a legal but moral responsibility to obey just laws. Conversely, one has a moral responsibility to disobey unjust laws. I would agree with Saint Augustine that "An unjust law is no law at all." Now what is the difference between the two? How does one determine when a law is just or unjust? A just law is a man-made code that squares with the moral law or the law of God. An unjust law is a code that is out of harmony with the moral law. To put it in the terms of Saint Thomas Aquinas, an unjust law is a human law that is not rooted in eternal and natural law...Of course there is nothing new about this kind of civil disobedience. It was seen sublimely in the refusal of Shadrach, Meshach, and Abednego to obey the laws of Nebuchadnezzar because a higher moral law was involved. It was practiced superbly by the early Christians who were willing to face hungry lions and the excruciating pain of chopping blocks, before submitting to certain unjust laws of the Roman Empire.

King is appealing to the highest law as the foundation for his moral crusade for racial equality. King took a stand that you almost never see today's conservative lawyers, activists, politicians, and organizations willing to take. Instead they often utilize the Left's language with statements like "the court struck down," and "the court legalized," or "the court's opinion is the law of the land," which accepts the immoral—dare we say pagan—legal positivistic philosophy of the very opponents they're contending with.

We need to follow King's lead. We need to be willing to say no. We will not comply. We will not do this. We will not participate in your long train of abuses and usurpations any longer. Call us every name you want. Broadcast all the fake news you want. Threaten us all you want.

We'll change our answer, all right. From no to hell no!

Find me one Republican in public office, just one, willing to lead this charge and you might get me to change my mind that we have no future in this party. But until you do, any good the good ones remaining might accomplish is a target to be nullified by a runaway tyrannical judiciary.

Any law they pass will be struck down shortly thereafter, if not used as a platform to implement the complete opposite at the whim of the judges.

Any vote you cast to "drain the swamp" is as productive as urinating into the wind, for the courts are the swamp's Navy SEALs, the first soldiers to rush into the battle on the swamp's behalf. It doesn't get any swampier than some unelected, pagan-educated elite with a lifetime appointment giving "we the people" the what-for.

Very few prominent voices in our movement will speak to this issue, beyond hand-wringing and cliché spewing. There's lots of potential reasons why this is the case, and they're all bad.

# Conservatism and Its Themes/ Values are More Popular Than Ever Before, So That Must Mean We're Winning

**TRUTH BOMB** *Audience does not equal influence.*

There's gold in them there hills.

We are selling more books than ever before. We are selling out more conferences than ever before. Fox News has become the number one network in all of cable television, regardless of format. In fact, there's so much demand for conservative content that more networks are emerging to fill the void, such as CRTV (where I work), One America News Network, *Newsmax*, and *Daily Wire*, and broadcasting giant Sinclair was also considering launching one of its own at the time this book was being written.

The most popular movies are borrowing liberally (see what I did there) from conservatism's ideals. For example, the super-villain Thanos in *Avengers: Infinity War* is basically the manifestation of the worldview of Margaret Sanger, the founder of Planned Parenthood. Gal Gadot's *Wonder Woman* favored

traditional complementary gender roles over third-wave femi-
nism, with the heroine basically offering herself up as a Christlike
redeemer battling Satan (packaged as the villain Ares) for the
souls of mankind. Even slacker films like *Knocked Up* have their
plots resolved by males living a prolonged adolescence deciding
to grow up, become men, get a real job, and take care of their
women and children.

Yet while conservatism is finding an audience, it's not
growing in influence. There is scant evidence that conservatism
is relevant when it comes to actual policy-making in places like
classrooms, courtrooms, boardrooms, newsrooms, or the halls of
Congress even when the Republicans are in charge.

To try and figure out why that is the case, for this chapter I
assembled a blue-ribbon panel of conservatives to answer five
questions about the state and future of the current conservative
movement. They are (in alphabetical order):

- **Glenn Beck:** A multiple *New York Times* bestselling
  author, founder of *The Blaze* news/opinion site, and one
  of the most successful broadcasters in the history of
  conservative media.
- **Erick Erickson:** Founder of *RedState* and *The Resurgent*
  and former CNN and Fox News contributor.
- **Daniel Horowitz:** Senior policy analyst for *Conservative
  Review*, whose past career in activism includes recruit-
  ing and equipping candidates for various conservative
  organizations.
- **Caleb Howe:** A prolific contributor to numerous top
  conservative sites and the former managing editor for
  *RedState*.

▶ **Ben Shapiro:** Arguably the most prominent voice in conservatism today, Shapiro is omnipresent in multimedia, runs the *Daily Wire*, and is a much in-demand speaker.

Here's how they answered the five questions I asked each of them in order to get their takes on where our movement really stands and where it's truly headed:

**Q: What do you think the country thinks conservatism is? Not what we think it is, but what do you think they think it is? And how do you think that should determine how we attempt to engage the culture?**

*BECK:* I think the general population thinks that conservatives are about big money and power and big military and war and corruption. To confront this, we have to be consistent, we have to be principled, and we have to be actively reaching out to people under thirty.

You can see in the way the media covered the move of our Israeli embassy to Jerusalem what we're up against. It was so clear that Hamas, a terrorist organization, was responsible for the deaths there. They were on television in the Middle East admitting it, and that they're going to kill all the Jews. How is our press not catching this? The answer is they are—they just don't care. They have their agenda. And I think a lot of people on our side saw this and likewise decided we don't care (about the truth) either and we have to win. But what we're failing to see is the next generation coming up doesn't buy into any of this. They don't want the Democrats and they don't want the Republicans. They're looking for something new, different, and has meaning. And right now, I'm not sure you find that much meaning in either the progressive or even the conservative point of view.

*ERICKSON:* I think the country looks at conservatism as a synonym for "Republican" and not as its own ideology or brand. And by being Republicans they mean "not the Democrats." I don't know that the public actually knows what conservatives stand for, or for that matter what Republicans stand for. And I think if we're going to successfully push back against the Left, it needs to revert to actually being about a battle of ideas and our ability to articulate those ideas.

*HOROWITZ:* On a fiscal level, most Americans genuinely think conservatism is about fiscal restraint. The problem is that although deep down they understand it's important, the emotional pull to government dependency often overpowers their better instincts on fiscal restraint. This is why conservatives need to do a better job explaining why progressivism created the fiscal pain of a higher cost of living in the first place. Most people see the high costs of health care and education and feel the pain. They want help. Nobody bothers to explain how big government policies created private "cartel" monopolies to gouge them, and how our policies would alleviate the burden by fostering choice and competition.

People understand market forces now more than they did in previous generations, because they understand the success of companies like Amazon and Apple. If we move beyond the mere concern of the cost of government programs, and explain how we are concerned about crony capitalism created by government monopolies, we will make in-roads—not among those who want free stuff at all costs, but with enough middle-of-the-road voters.

Which brings me to cultural issues. The Left is so extreme that they no longer believe in X and Y chromosomes. Yet, they have succeeded in painting us as wild-eyed Iranian theocrats who want to install cameras in their bedrooms and confiscate their sacred sex toys. So, the country thinks we are the crazies.

By actually being consistent on economic liberties and showing how we are the champions of hands-off liberties, and that the Rainbow Jihad are the ones who are the true theocrats who want to coerce their virtues, we can successfully rebrand the battle to defend traditional values.

*HOWE:* It seems to me that conservatism is not used to describe a political philosophy anymore, but rather, when used at all, to describe a type of person. In the general popular sense, a conservative is someone who thinks that Obama was bad, Bush was good, war is good, taxes are bad, rich people are good, poor people are bad, and white people are better than nonwhite people. This perception is of course inaccurate and entirely a shame, and conservatives have an equal responsibility for this perception as the media has.

People should see the conservative philosophy as one that resists change for change's sake, that resists increasing government power because it reduces individual liberty, and of course, yes, abhors taxes as a necessary evil. Conservatives should be perceived as, and should be, those who despise racism as backward and detrimental, and love capitalism as evenhanded and beneficial.

Most importantly, though, it should be the perception that a conservative, like their liberal counterparts, is someone who wants what is best, who wants the thing that gives the greatest benefit to the largest number of people at the least inconvenience and the lowest societal cost. They simply have different ways of achieving those ends than liberals have. I don't know that there is any possible strategy for changing popular perception on these points. But with regard to engaging the culture, I think absolutely that the "perception" should be a factor in every interaction, inasmuch as that consideration does not abrogate the actual intended effect of conservative policy.

*SHAPIRO:* In order to determine what the country thinks it is, you have to define who you're talking about in the country because obviously those are widely disparate views. If you're the normal person on the Left, they think conservatism is reactionary racism, cruelty to the poor, and all the myths about conservatism taught in the media and academia. If you're talking about the general public or the typical person who voted for Donald Trump in 2016, I'm not sure they have a perception of the so-called conservative movement. I'm not sure the conservative movement is an intellectually coherent thing for most people who vote. Those discussing what the conservative movement is tend to be inside the conservative movement, and for those people outside of the conservative movement they don't think anything of it.

The real question is if there's a conservative movement that is generating conservative politics, or is it just a weird conglomeration of people who voted for a particular candidate. I think at the moment it's probably the latter. I think the intellectualization of the Trump movement is far-fetched. I think a lot of people with different policy opinions on issues like tariffs voted for Trump for different reasons—like Hillary Clinton stunk.

**Q: What is the current state of "conservative media" and what, if anything, would you change about it if you could?**

*BECK:* I think the state of conservative media is very bad. It's hemorrhaging, and there is no exit strategy. You know, you could start the progressive Huffington Post and sell it to Time Warner for a billion dollars. So you can find investors on their side. That doesn't exist on the Right. Nobody will buy our media companies, except the true believers. This makes it very difficult to create another Fox News, and Fox News is under attack like nobody's business. It's all guns ablaze on Fox News. Then, if you look at the new media Facebook and YouTube, and how their algorithms are changing, I know people across the ideological spectrum are seeing their views and clicks way down. When it comes to conservative media, we either need to hang together or we will hang separately. We've got to come together and start watching each other's backs, because they're picking us off one by one.

*ERICKSON:* Conservative media is too entangled with the Trump administration, just as mainstream media is too entangled with the Democrats, so people aren't getting the full picture. I think we could actually influence public policy better if we had the full picture, as opposed to what gets painted by much of conservative media. I think it gets dumbed down to the point of cheerleading, as if everything the GOP does is right, and not everything they do is right. Nor is it always just the Democrats' fault every time something goes wrong. There are a lot of Republicans out there who are spending more than they should, while claiming to be for small government.

Because conservatism has just become a flank of the Republican Party, we don't hear about those Republicans who are helping the Democrats bankrupt the country.

*HOROWITZ:* Conservative media is just as broken as the Republican Party. You can only have a Republican Party committing political adultery every day for thirty years if the conservative "spouse" is at peace with it. Conservative media suffers from its own form of an opioid crisis. They get high on the political morphine of taking selfies on Fox News and making money from commentating as an end to itself.

Thus, they are not seeking solutions to overturn the system because they are making too much money off the system. The lynchpin is, as always, money. There is no money inherent in standing for principle.

The good news is that, in this era, the bar to entry into the public square is so much lower. It doesn't take much for someone with passion and knowledgeable ideas to obtain a following at a relatively low cost. But the key is to find a landing place for these emerging voices so that they don't fall victim to the curse of success in this business. Once an anti-system voice tends to reach the tipping point of success, he gets co-opted by the system because that is the only place to make real money and advance to the next level. Conservatives need to invade that next tier or risk losing their farm team like drinking coffee with a fork.

*HOWE:* Conservative media is in a confused state. It is hard for any politically partisan media to survive its own success, and in the case of conservative media and Trump, that is especially true. Considering that the success of Trump came at the expense of genuine conservatives, and that his governance, while achieving some conservative goals, has not in character or tone presented a conservative philosophy. And considering that the popular culture's embrace of Trumpism as indistinguishable from conservatism has watered down and misbranded the philosophy itself, the media dedicated to advancing that philosophy finds itself on perilous footing. Should we be propping him up? Tearing him down? Calling balls and strikes? None of these are obvious answers, and none once decided upon easy to implement.

If I could change one thing about "conservative media," it would be to make it more tolerant of the current fractured state rather than fighting it. This would mean funding from activist donors who want to encourage the exposure of multiple points of view, rather than consolidating behind a particular one.

*SHAPIRO:* There are a couple of different angles to this question. Number one, how much is the conservative media reliant on certain gatekeepers like Facebook and YouTube to gather traffic? The state of conservatism is the best it's ever been, and we're generating a ton of traffic. But a lot of companies like ours are very reliant on social media platform distribution to draw traffic. And if those companies turned off the spigot, that would have a very ugly impact on us business-wise.

More generally, conservative media has been fractured by the emergence of Trump. Which is weird to me, because if you're really a conservative you should agree on a lot of the same things (to conserve). Trump does some things that aren't conservative, and he does some things that are conservative. We're not asking every day whether you'd vote for him today, we're asking whether he's doing something conservative. So we should all have largely the same take on that. If he does something conservative, great, and he if does something stupid we chide him.

Beyond that, there are too many members of the conservative media who have fallen into the trap that everything Trump does is great because it ticks off the Left, or everything Trump does is bad because he fails at one or other particular area. Not everything in conservative media should revolve around Trump either way, but unfortunately, I kind of think it does. He's become the star in which we all revolve.

**Q: What is the status and future of the relationship between conservatism and the Republican Party?**

*BECK:* I don't think the Republicans or the Democrats have much of a future. Just like the Democrats became about Barack Obama, and at the time that worked for them but now it doesn't, the Republicans are now all Donald Trump. That may be good right now, but it's not good for the future. And if it's not Donald Trump, then it's GOP leaders in Congress, who are much worse. At least Donald Trump is doing something in foreign policy; what was the GOP Congress doing all this time? I don't even know what the Republicans even stand for.

If we're going to survive as a country, conservatives need to be the ones who say, "Let's preserve the things that we know work and are good." For instance, the Constitution, which embodies the principles that we know work. Let's get rid of all the other stuff that we know doesn't work. If we return to those roots, and we link arms with those who are effective at going to colleges and reaching those under thirty, then I think conservatism has a real chance. But I don't think it has any chance with the Republican Party in the long run.

*ERICKSON:* Hopefully there will be a disentangling. It began after George W. Bush nominated Harriet Miers for the US Supreme Court, which produced the first conservative media revolt against a betrayal by the GOP. Unfortunately, a lot of conservative media has decided to loop back in as cheerleaders, this time for the Trump administration. My hope is the conservative movement will reclaim its roots rather than remain a cheerleader for a political party.

*HOROWITZ:* So long as conservatives call the GOP home, conservatism will continue to slide to the left. Given that Democrats move light years to the left every year, and Republicans only exist to be "not the Democrats," the GOP is schlepped along for the ride. Given that conservatism, at its current state, exists to validate where the GOP is at the given moment relative to Democrats, they will continue to make the leftward journey. Unless a new party and a new movement is created, we will see conservatism in ten years being defined by only supporting one sex change operation per family instead of two and government-sponsored family trips every six months, albeit with tenuous work requirements that can be waived by the states.

There is a reason we are where we are—it's the same reason we will continue to languish unless an external force is applied of at least equal and opposing force. Newton's laws of motion apply to politics. We will not succeed with just a few voices in the wilderness trying to change institutions. Even if we successfully elect them, they will get co-opted by the system.

With Newton's second law of motion, the movement of an object is dependent upon two variables—the force acting upon the object and the mass of the object itself. Until we have a new movement of equal size opposing the system with greater velocity than what is propelling it in the wrong direction, things will not change. The laws of politics are nearly identical to the laws of velocity and inertia.

HOWE: The Republican Party remains the only home for conservatives, but it is not a good home. There is no air-conditioning, the windows are broken, and everyone sleeps on the floor. It would be a better home if some repair work were done, but that doesn't seem likely. The future for the party is, I think, increased apathy for their candidates and the races. There is an extent to which one must ask oneself how long they intend to vote for someone who isn't going to do the things one wants done anyway. I know in my own case, I wonder how much effort and loyalty I'm willing to expend on a party that I think betrayed us in the primary of 2016 and hasn't done anything of especially significant value to change that betrayal. Some scraps have come in 2017 and 2018, but hardly enough to make this a good and happy relationship. It's contentious. It will probably remains so for the foreseeable future.

SHAPIRO: I think the future of the Republican Party depends on its leadership. It's just a vehicle. If anyone says they're a Republican before a conservative, does that mean they'd support anything the party does? If you're a conservative first, then that simply means right now the Republican Party is your best vehicle for creating political change along the lines you're looking for. Right now, Trump is the de facto leader of the Republican Party, but he isn't its thought leader. So we should hold him accountable just like GOP leadership in Congress. It's struggling to represent its base because its base is so far-flung and disparate. And as long as that continues, I think it will be very difficult for the Republican Party to continue winning.

**Q: If you could remove one influence/fad/trend/conventional wisdom from conservatism, what would it be and why?**

BECK: This is a hard one. I would say that I would remove the concept that God is on our side and replace it with we wanna make sure we're on His side. We just count He's on our side because of things like abortion. But that's us going on His side. Are we always trying to be on His side?

We have this really weird thing about us as conservatives, because we're considered the torchbearer for faith, and yet I think we lack in faith. We look to men and to tricks and everything else to get things done. And we shouldn't, but remain worthy of blessing. Strengthen that inner voice, which we are going to need with the types of technology coming our way. We're going to need a deep connection to the Spirit. The only way to do so is to listen to it and obey it. And the voice gets stronger the more we do, especially when you do what it says when it doesn't make much sense.

We need to trust in God. We were a country founded on divine providence. Let's find our sacred honor again. Be humble and trust that liberty is only going to go away if we betray it, because we won't deserve it.

*ERICKSON:* The idea we should rally around individuals instead of ideas. I'm old enough to remember when conservatives mocked Democrats for creating a cult of personality around Barack Obama. This is not even a Trump point. There's a field of elected Republicans out there that we tend to rally behind instead of ideas. We need to rally around ideas instead. People are flawed, therefore even the best idea can be brought down by a corrupted soul, when we make it about personalities instead of ideas.

*HOROWITZ:* I'd purge the Koch addiction on the Right. The Koch brothers are a cancer on conservatism—plain and simple. Remember, money is the mother's milk of politics. There is almost no money on the Right over and beyond the traditional special interests and industries that donate to establishment Republicans, many of which also donate to Democrats. The Kochs are the only George Soros-level funders of groups associated more with the "conservative movement"—over and beyond (and even sometimes against) the GOP establishment.

Yet, the Kochs have accepted the entire de-civilization agenda of the Left. They believe in the Rainbow Jihad, are rabidly open borders, are warm to Islamism, and are getting every conservative ally we have in Washington addicted to the Willie Horton agenda on crime. We cannot recover from a movement whose largest donors believe in the most radical and destructive agenda items of the other side.

What is ironic and disconcerting is that it's not like we are witnessing some amazing free market libertarian revolution on fiscal issues as a result of their libertarian influence. We incur the pain of their stinger, but are never entreated to the taste of the honey. They have only shown their effectiveness when they join with the Left on civilization issues, not when they clash with them on economic issues.

Because, let's face it, even as it relates to economic issues, they are not driven by godly principles but by self-interest that happens to overlap with some of our principles. If we can only win by being led by Koch conservatism, then there is nothing left to fight for. There is no way to have a small "g" God without the capital "G" government they claim to oppose. There is no way to have open borders, criminal anarchy from jailbreak, and the promotion of political Islam while living with prosperity and free enterprise. Just ask the Romans. We can only actualize, "And they shall dwell each man under his vine and under his fig tree" (Micah 4:4), when we will say, "Come, let us go up to the Lord's mount and to the house of the God of Jacob, and let Him teach us of His ways, and we will go in His paths" (Micah 4:2).

*HOWE:* This is a tough one. I would probably wish away the notion that people who are soft on immigration are evil traitors to Republican-kind. Or the truly willfully blind idea that there is no significant amount of racism in the world, that there is no such thing as institutional racism, or that addressing race is not in the interest of the party. These issues also call back to your first question about perception.

*SHAPIRO:* This one is pretty easy—that "owning the libs" is the greatest thing possible. That should not be our goal. The goal should be to speak truth, and then if that offends the Left that's fine. It's just the truth. Unfortunately, I think a lot of people on the Right have been seduced by this trend that if it ticks off the Left then it's good. Well, that could eventually drive you into some pretty nasty territory because there are a lot of things that tick off the Left that actually are not that good. You can say a lot of nasty or untoward things to tick off the Left you wouldn't even say in the privacy of your home, and then justify it because "if it made somebody on the Left mad that's good." It's not self-justifying just to do or say something because it made people on the Left mad.

**Q: What is the future of conservatism and the country? Are you optimistic or pessimistic about where we're headed?**

*BECK:* I am very optimistic actually. There's something happening, and believe it or not, it's happening first with those who are actually liberal. They may have thought they were progressive, but now they're smart enough to know there's a difference. As progressivism has gone off the rails, and we've moved into postmodernism where there is no truth, just your truth and my truth—and even that is imaginary. As that train has come off the tracks, deep thinkers on the Left I talk to are more afraid of that viewpoint than they are of ours.

That doesn't mean they're conservatives. Just that they're saying, "Wait a minute, this doesn't make any sense. You're disconnecting from science and any kind of fact. You're turning on everybody, and this isn't going to last long." I think people are sensing, in an American sort of way, what I think Thomas Paine was thinking when he saw the guillotines come out in the French Revolution: uh-oh, wait a minute, this is going wrong. I think we have a real opportunity to be reasonable and sit down and talk logic and facts, without arrogance, and perhaps restore the Bill of Rights.

If we could just restore the Bill of Rights, and agree to never go off it, we cure much of what ails us.

It's healthy for us as conservatives to have this conversation and take stock in who we are and what it is we're trying to win. But we really should take solace in how far left the Democratic Party is going and say, "Oh man, I'm glad I'm not them."

*ERICKSON:* I'm a natural-born pessimist, so I'm typically pessimistic about everything. But I'm actually optimistic about the future of conservatism. The main reason for my optimism is that we are blessed by foolish opponents on the Left, who have had to rebrand themselves several times already.

We will get through this age. Maybe not advancing all of the same ideas, but ultimately conservatism should be, and will return to be, about the empowerment of individuals against the government Leviathan.

*HOROWITZ:* There is an old Jewish saying: "The salvation of God is like the blink of an eye." Nothing is permanent in this world, and we can certainly see that in this era of instant communication where one day's news cycle is the equivalent of a month's news cycle of yesteryear. God provides us with many challenges and opportunities on a geopolitical level to do the right thing. Furthermore, the breathtaking velocity of the extremism on the Left always provides us with the opportunity to draw a sharp contrast. Many of our colleagues believe we have lost the culture and even the demographics. That might be true, but most voters sure as heck are not where the Democratic Party wants to take us. Most people are still not champions of Hamas, Hezbollah, MS-13, drug cartels, and Willie Horton-like criminals that are coddled by the Left. I'm, therefore, optimistic about the opportunities ahead inasmuch as our doom is not immutable or inevitable.

But whether we have a movement in place to seize that opportunity is up to us and will depend upon whether "our people" wake up and recognize that what we are doing is not working. I suspect things will have to first get worse before that happens. Israel has now reached the point where the founding Labor Party has been destroyed and it seems that the Right has created a permanent governing majority. But that only happened after the Left in Israel was allowed to take their country to the brink, with thousands killed and thousands forcibly uprooted from their homes after their land was handed over to Hamas. Then the people woke up.

Will we have to suffer some equivalent catharsis before the radicalism of the Left is evident enough, and those on the Right get their act together? That is the million-dollar question.

*HOWE:* As for the future I truly cannot say. At this populist moment, the ideals and values of conservatives are openly mocked by both the Left and the extreme Right. It is a back-seat philosophy right now, and the things necessary to change that seem impossible from where we sit. Perhaps that is pessimistic, perhaps merely an observation. I am by nature optimistic about the American spirit and the country as a whole. But I can admit to some pessimism about the short-term (twenty years) prospects in this country politically. It is not going to be a priority for the Republican Party to cater to the conservative worldview for some time. If nothing else, that is a reason for pessimism about how well or quickly the country can recover from the last decade.

*SHAPIRO*: I'm optimistic because I think the Left has overreached dramatically. Their identity politics, intolerance, and desire to box everybody into this tiny Overton window of acceptable discourse I think is failing. I think a lot of people are looking for answers, and there's a feeling the government is too big and bothering all of us too much, so you're seeing this surge of libertarianism among younger people. So I'm optimistic there could really be some good discussions happening, thanks to the overreach by the Left. But that's going to require some leadership politically and intellectually inside the conservative movement, and I'm hoping we can have those discussions.

\* \* \* \* \*

The answers you just read were printed as given, so these were entirely the thoughts of our distinguished panel. For that reason, I will also take a pass on commenting on their answers. That way they will stand on their own and you, the reader, can consider them for yourself.

Also, none of our panelists were informed about the answers given by their peers beforehand. So nobody compared any notes or preemptively sought to fashion a narrative. We did it that way to avoid creating a feedback loop, and so they would each feel free to share their own individual thoughts.

# The Three Rs: Revival, Rules for Patriots, and Revolution

If you've made it this far, congratulations! You've earned your critical thinker merit badge and proven yourself to be a patriot. Not because you agree with everything I've said up until this point, but simply because you were willing to consider it.

I like winning arguments, but I like starting them even more. We don't always have to agree, but we'd be wise to usually listen and assess before deciding whether or not we do. Our major problem in this country is not that we're arguing too much—it's that we're really not arguing at all.

We're trolling each other with the most vicious personal language possible, then retreating to our own bubbles and echo chambers where we say even nastier things about "the other" to the like-minded and calling that an argument.

That's not an argument any more than gossiping about so-and-so at church is seeking prayer requests. That's the kind of passive-aggressive back stabbing that causes a culture to implode, which ours is on the verge of if we're not careful.

Therefore, let me first thank you for considering the truths contained in this book, and conclude by offering some potential guidance on what to do with that knowledge you're now armed with.

I don't want you to walk away from this book believing there's no hope, because that's not my intended message. I'm a Christian, so I *never* believe in the absence of hope. I have a worldview that begins with the premise a sovereign God supernaturally intervened in human history to raise His once dead son back to life, after he was tortured to death on a cross and buried in a tomb behind a one-ton rock.

But then God rolled that stone away and His one and only son, Jesus Christ, got up and walked out of that tomb three days later like a boss.

When your entire belief system is based on a resurrection, hopelessness isn't an option. So there's always hope, especially when you're a conservative. Because you only become a conservative by looking at what HIStory has revealed to be worthy of conserving. Thus, true conservatives are *always* on the right side of history.

That means it's not our principles that need to be reevaluated if we're not having the cultural impact we desire, but our tactics and attachments. This book has clearly proven our current tactical paradigm and unconditional attachment to the Republican Party is a loser. We are being set up to fail, regardless of the outcome of elections, because we are aligned with people who don't believe the same things we do.

The Republican Party, as it's currently constructed, is a bridge to nowhere. No matter how much we dominate its grassroots, we are dramatically outnumbered among its leadership who calls the shots. At best we are slowing the rate of leftist progressive growth. However, we are not turning back the rising neo-Marxist tide despite all the elections Republicans have won in recent cycles, let alone moving the country to the right by any objective measure.

If you keep doing what you've always done, you'll keep getting the same results you always have. Considering our children's futures are at stake, as is the future of the greatest country in the history of creation, maintaining the status quo is simply not an option, as this book has made plain.

Moving forward, I believe we have three alternative paths to thwarting American exceptionalism's road to perdition—or reverse our ominous cultural trend lines, and get beyond the unibrow party duopoly paradigm that fights us harder than they pretend to fight each other.

They are what I call the three Rs: Revival, Rules for Patriots, and Revolution.

## Revival

It must begin here because as Founding Father John Adams once said, "Our Constitution was made only for a moral and religious people. It is wholly inadequate to the government of any other."[1]

It's not a mystery why the colonies had spiritual Great Awakenings and *then* fought for their freedom. It's actually basic cultural math. A people freed from the tyranny of their own sin will then desire to be freed of the sins of the tyrant ruling over them. Once our relationship with our Maker is restored, we will have less appetite to be ruled by mere mortals who possess the same frailties as we do.

The math works in reverse as well.

The more detached we are from our God, the more government will fill that void. As G. K. Chesterton put it, "Once abolish the God and the government becomes the god."[2] Furthermore, the more immoral a people become the more government must grow to account for their misdeeds. More laws are needed as we devise new and creative ways to act out our fallen nature and basic instincts, inflicting suffering upon our fellow man. More laws require more government officials to interpret and enforce them. Since those working in government are just as fallen as the rest of us, they're also temptable and corruptible, which then requires more laws to regulate their misbehaving, too. As it becomes more and more obvious those charged with protecting us from ourselves are just as susceptible to the human condition as the general population, distrust of government will mount.

This is where we are now.

We have lost trust in the institutions once meant to hold the line and protect us from ourselves. For example, our government spies on every American, yet ignores multiple warnings of looming mass shooters in schools and nightclubs. The neighborhood beat cop has been replaced by someone who looks outfitted for *Call of Duty*. Police brutality and violent acts targeting police are simultaneous societal ills. Journalism as a profession, freed by the First Amendment to hold the system accountable and speak truth to power, is all but gone now. The church is now seen more as an instrument of political partisanship than a transcendent witness to the moral high ground. On any given day the Constitution may mean something totally different depending on what the most recent court ruling says, and then that ruling may be overruled the very next day.

This is why litigious societies *always* devolve into lawless ones, because the same corruption within a culture that dooms it to being weighed down by burdensome laws and regulations cannot be fixed by them. It doesn't correct the corruption but amplifies it like a feedback loop. Wrong begets more wrong because wickedness cannot curse wickedness. Beelzebub cannot cast out Beelzebub. Disease doesn't cure disease. What do you get when you multiply zero times zero?

Zero.

Thus, any strategy we as conservatives seek to save this nation we love must start here with revival, or it will end before it ever started.

So pray for revival, like my friend Bob Vander Plaats does. He's got an alarm on his phone that goes off at 7:14 every day in honor of Second Chronicles 7:14: "If my people, which are called by my name, shall humble themselves, and pray, and seek my face, and turn from their wicked ways; then will I hear from heaven, and will forgive their sin, and will heal their land."

God did not speak those words for twenty-first century America. He spoke them to ancient Israel. Still, God is the same yesterday, today, and forever. The same heart He had for those who believed in Him back then He still has for those who will believe in Him now. This is why I end my show every day with a reference to Jesus's words in John 3:17: "For God did not send His Son into the world to condemn the world, *but so that through him the world may be saved.*"

It was only with "a firm reliance upon divine providence" that this nation was forged, and only by returning to that creed shall it be conserved. With God, all things are possible. But without Him, all we are is dust in the wind, dude.

## Rules for Patriots

I believe in fighting like it's up to us and praying like it's up to Him.

I also believe we can walk and chew gum at the same time.

So while we're praying for and seeking out revival, we must fight hard. But we must also fight smart. Conservatives' current tactical array is woefully underwhelming, consisting mostly of "owning the libs" like this is nothing more than a rap battle from *8 Mile*. Barney Fife was more dangerous with his one bullet.

If I could summarize conservative strategy during my time in politics, I would use a famous quip from football coaching legend John McKay. When asked once about how inept his team's offensive execution was, he deadpanned, "Our offensive execution? I'm in favor of it."[3]

It would take an entire book to correct all the tactical mistakes we have made as a movement. Which is exactly why I already wrote it—and it's called *Rules for Patriots: How Conservatives Can Win Again*. It's been endorsed by everyone from President Trump to original Never Trumper Erick Erickson, because there's never been a book like it before or since. Instead of simply another tome explaining why the Left are a bunch of losers, I decided to lay out a plan for how we might finally stop being the gang who couldn't shoot straight. After all, if the Left sucks as much as we say, what does it say about us that we've lost our culture to those guys?

So go to Amazon.com right now and buy a copy. Put those "10 Commandments of Political Warfare" that are the heart of the book into practice. Stop taking their crap and start taking back ground.

## Revolution

Now we come to the moment of critical mass.

Since by now I've made it clear I love sports analogies, particularly those involving football, permit me to make one more. When the clock is ticking down to its final seconds in a close game, and there's only enough time for one more play, the coach that's behind on the scoreboard may call for what's known as a "Hail Mary."

It's a play born out of a legendary 1975 NFL playoff game between the Dallas Cowboys and Minnesota Vikings.[4] Trailing in the final minute, Dallas's Hall of Fame quarterback, Roger Staubach, called for wide receiver Drew Pearson to just run down the field as far as he could. Staubach would then heave the ball to him in the hopes of scoring a miraculous game-winning touchdown.

The play was nicknamed "the Hail Mary" because the devoutly religious Staubach admitted to saying a Hail Mary prayer just as he launched the pass. Thus, from that time forward, whenever a football team uses the same play to successfully snatch victory from the jaws of defeat in the final seconds, it is known as "the Hail Mary."

The Hail Mary is the endgame play, only to be used when the more conventional means of winning are no longer attainable, because there's simply not enough time remaining to gradually work the ball down the field. It's at that point the head coach will call for the play, since any risk involved is outweighed by what's at stake. You're at critical mass, hence you have no choice but to go all in, pour all your chips into the middle of the poker table, and make your final stand here.

I believe we are at that stage of the game when it comes to our Constitution, which is the bedrock of our republic.

# CONCLUSION

The Republican Party, at best, is a blunt instrument to stall the Left's ultimate victory long enough to give us a chance to stop it. At worse, it is aiding and abetting the Left's quest. Which leaves us with no real political representation.

At the same time the courts are completely gone—becoming the Left's primary weapon of mass destruction they use to unravel our Constitution.

Then there's academia, which has become the leftist progressives' youth ministry. Churning out new generations of voters year after year, either ignorant of or hostile to what our Constitution stands for.

Our Constitution is, in a word, besieged.

We are cut off from all traditional methods of passing onto our children what historian Cleon Skousen once described as "a miracle that changed the world."[5] The clock is ticking. The First and Second Amendments that define its fundamental mission are facing the full onslaught of the Left. Our Constitution is hanging by a thread. And if it goes, so goes American exceptionalism.

It's time to call for the Hail Mary.

In this realm, that Hail Mary is what's known as the "Article 5 Convention of States." It's a somewhat obscure provision embedded in the Constitution by our founding fathers so we could fight another revolution if need be, except this time minus the bloodshed they could not avoid with theirs.

If revival is the soul of American exceptionalism, revolution is the heart. For there is no more revolutionary notion in this world than there is a God, and our rights come from Him and not government. And that means government's only real role in our lives is to protect and preserve those God-given rights, not to play god in our lives.

Except for this nation, this revolutionary notion has never really existed in the course of human events. We have managed to hold on to it when other cultures could not, and we largely have our Constitution to thank for that. Which is exactly why it's under attack from those who desire to recreate the Bolshevik Revolution instead.

The Convention of States Project is the tip of the spear here, and has been steadfastly working to get enough states across the country to sign off on calling for an Article 5 Convention since 2013.[6] Its motivations are uniquely American, and come straight from the writings and words of the founding fathers themselves:

> To bring power back to the states and the people, where it belongs. Unelected bureaucrats in Washington, D.C. shouldn't be allowed to make sweeping decisions that impact millions of Americans. But right now, they do. So it all boils down to one question: Who do you think should decide what's best for you and your family? You, or the feds?
>
> We'd vote for the American people every single time.

It's almost like you can hear the late, great William F. Buckley's famous line, "I'd rather be governed by the first two thousand names in the Boston telephone directory than by the two thousand people on the faculty at Harvard" after reading that![7]

Now, should the thirty-four required number of states agree to call for an Article 5 Convention of States, the convention would be focused on the following:

> Our convention would only allow the states to discuss amendments that "limit the power and jurisdiction of the federal government, impose fiscal restraints, and place term limits on federal officials."

This is what separates an Article 5 Convention from the far riskier full-blown constitutional convention. The latter could absolutely devolve into a free-for-all, with forces out to dismantle our Constitution once and for all using it as the platform to deliver the kill shot. However, an Article 5 Convention of States can only be called to specifically address the purposes clearly defined in the resolutions passed by the required thirty-four states. And then it comes with a further fail-safe—even more states, thirty-eight, would be required to ratify any amendments it proposes.

Of course, despite such fail-safes a Convention of States is not absent any risk, which is why I wouldn't have supported such an effort ten to twenty years ago. But we're at the point of the game now that just allowing the clock to run out while we're behind on the scoreboard is an existential risk. It means the game goes final, the Constitution loses, and American exceptionalism is lost along with it. And once the game goes final, it cannot be replayed. It goes down in the books in permanent marker.

If you think we're not at such a critical mass, then you and I clearly aren't seeing the same things. Chances are, though, if you made it all the way to the end of the book, you also believe we're at such a critical mass—whether or not you agree with all my observations and analysis.

Therefore, I urge you to join our effort to call an Article 5 Convention of States. The Convention of States Project can be reached online at www.conventionofstates.com. COS is standing tall in the pocket like any good quarterback, ready to throw the ball into the end zone in the hopes of pulling the game out. All they need is for "we the people" to be stationed down there waiting to catch it.

* * * * *

I close now with this: I never intended to write another political book. I'd all but given up on my politics as my life's work, believing the system to be too far gone. Recent works like Rod Dreher's *The Benedict Option*, which essentially calls for a modern monastic movement to preserve our virtue while American culture careens irredeemably over the cliff, appeal to my overall cynicism regarding the state of things.

But one day out of the blue the outline of this book came to me, and what also came to me is that while there are plenty of reasons to give up on the system, there is never a reason for us to give up on each other. I serve a Lord who died for me while I was his enemy. I'm commanded to love my neighbor as I love myself. I'm to emulate a Savior who impractically leaves ninety-nine behind to find just the one lost sheep.

This book, then, is the result of giving it one more try. To see if there are enough of us remaining truly willing to do what it takes to win, because we know what winning really means. It doesn't mean clicks or careers; it means conserving for this and future generations the last, best hope for mankind east of Eden.

The harvest is plenty, but the workers are few. It's time to find out if the Lord of the harvest is still sending out workers to tend to His fields here in this land that I love. Or if He is commanding folks like me to kick the dust off our sandals and move on. For the same Lord who doesn't give up on people will respect the wishes of people who freely choose to give up on Him.

So just as the Convention of States is our Constitution's Hail Mary pass, on a personal level this book is mine. To discern whether it's time to say "here I stand" like Martin Luther once did to change human history, or whether it's time to flee from the abomination of desolation as Christ warned.

The answer to that question now lies in your hands.

# Endnotes

## Introduction

1 Conservative Review staff, "Liberty Scores," *Conservative Review*, accessed July 3, 2018.

## Lie #1

1 Family Guardian Fellowship, "Thomas Jefferson On Politics & Government," 13. Political Parties, Family Guardian, accessed July 3, 2018, https://famguardian.org/Subjects/Politics/ThomasJefferson/jeff0800.htm.
2 Withoutbleeding, "Thelma & Louise: Ending Scene," Youtube video, 1:24, August 3, 2007, https://www.youtube.com/watch?v=4z88U915uq8.
3 ABC News, "Mitt Romney: Trump 'A Con Man, a Fake' [FULL SPEECH]," Youtube video, 17:25, March 3, 2016, https://www.youtube.com/watch?v=0xd3kr-QpeM.
4 The Political Mashups Team, "WATCH: Romney Agrees with Obama…On Everything," *HuffPost* video, last modified October 23, 2012, https://www.huffingtonpost.com/2012/10/22/romney-obama-debate_n_2004105.html.
5 Rachel Weiner, "McCain Calls Paul, Cruz, Amash 'Wacko Birds,'" *The Washington Post*, March 8, 2013, https://www.washingtonpost.com/news/post-politics/wp/2013/03/08/mccain-calls-paul-cruz-amash-wacko-birds/?utm_term=.41ce76f62eda.
6 Tasha Diakides, "McCain to Crowd: 'Don't Be Scared' of Obama Presidency," *CNN Politics*, October 11, 2008, http://politicalticker.blogs.cnn.com/2008/10/11/mccain-to-crowd-dont-be-scared-of-obama-presidency/.
7 Michael Saul, "Obama: Some Pennsylvanians 'Bitter,'" *Daily News*, April 12, 2008, http://www.nydailynews.com/news/politics/obama-pennsylvanians-bitter-article-1.283600.
8 Steven Ertelt, "Obama Admin Tells Supreme Court: Force Catholic nuns to Obey Birth Control Mandate," *Life News*, January 3, 2014, http://www.lifenews.com/2014/01/03/obama-admin-tells-supreme-court-force-catholic-nuns-to-obey-birth-control-mandate/.
9 Katie Sanders, "Have Democrats Lost 900 Seats in State Legislatures Since Obama Has Been President?" *Politifact*, January 25, 2015, http://www.politifact.com/punditfact/statements/2015/jan/25/cokie-roberts/have-democrats-lost-900-seats-state-legislatures-o/.
10 Rod Anderson, "Is Trump Nebuchadnezzar—and Does That Mean You Should Vote for Him?" *The Christian Post*, July 25, 2016, http://www.politifact.com/punditfact/statements/2015/jan/25/cokie-roberts/have-democrats-lost-900-seats-state-legislatures-o/.

11  Steve Deace, "The Democrat Convention: As Pagan as They Wanna Be," *Townhall*, September 8, 2012, http://www.politifact.com/punditfact /statements/2015/jan/25/cokie-roberts/have-democrats-lost-900-seats-state -legislatures-o/.

## Lie #2

1  Alex Swoyer, "Donald Trump Hires Three Key Advisors in Iowa, Expands His Reach," *Breitbart*, April 7, 2015, https://www.breitbart.com/big-government /2015/04/07/donald-trump-hires-three-key-advisors-in-iowa-expands-his-reach/.

2  Deace, "Donald Trump a Typical New York City Liberal Then and Now," *Conservative Review*, January 18, 2016, https://www.conservativereview.com/ news/donald-trump-a-typical-new-york-city-liberal-then-and-now/.

3  David A. Fahrenthold, "Mitt Romney Reframes Himself as a 'Severely Conservative' Governor," *The Washington Post*, February 16, 2012, https:// www.washingtonpost.com/politics/mitt-romney-reframes-himself-as -a-severely-conservative-governor/2012/02/14/gIQAaMiqHR_story.html?noredirect=on&utm_term=.d26ed9513037.

4  Les Grossman NEW OFFICIAL CHANNEL, "Donald Trump: McCain's a War Hero Because He Was Captured, 'I Like People That Weren't,'" Youtube video, 6:49, July 18, 2015, https://www.youtube.com/watch?v=7k1ajHAeXMU.

5  Les Grossman NEW OFFICIAL CHANNEL, "Donald Trump: 'I'm Not Sure I Have' Ever Asked God for Forgiveness,'" Youtube video, 2:28, July 18, 2015, https://www.youtube.com/watch?v=NyDbOHvfdiE.

6  Evan Carmichael, "Never, EVER, GIVE UP!"—Donald Trump (@realDonald-Trump) Top 10 Rules," Youtube video, 17:41, June 30, 3017, https://www. youtube.com/watch?v=rI4l4wcSS2w.

7  FilMagicians, "Orson Welles Talks Touch of Evil, James Cagney & Jean Renoir," Youtube video, 13:14, October 1, 2017, https://www.youtube.com/ watch?v=niMGXhS28YI.

8  Deace, "2016 Iowa Caucuses: Did Trump Implode, Has Jindal Arrived?" *The Washington Times*, July 20, 2015, https://www.washingtontimes.com/ news/2015/jul/20/steve-deace-2016-iowa-caucuses-did-trump-implode-h/.

9  Donald Trump, "Trump: I Don't Need to Be Lectured," *USA Today*, July 19, 2015, https://www.usatoday.com/story/opinion/2015/07/19/donald-trump-republican-party-presidential-candidate-editorials-debates/30389993/.

10  Deace, *Rules for Patriots: How Conservatives Can Win Again* (New York: Post Hill Press, 2016).

11  "Trump Attacks Ben Carson, Mocks Stabbing Story," *The Wall Street Journal*, November 13, 2015, https://www.wsj.com/video/trump-attacks-ben-carson-mocks-stabbing-story/1300D28F-9486-4D81-BC70-89B3155C241E.html.

12 Katie Glueck, "Ben Carson's Perplexing Stance on Abortion," *Politico*, August 18, 2015, https://www.politico.com/story/2015/08/ben-carson-abortion-stance-121456.

13 Chris Riotta, "Here Are the Best Memes and Jokes on Chris Christie's Awkward Super Tuesday Face," *Yahoo*, March 2, 2016, https://www.yahoo.com/news/best-memes-jokes-chris-christies-170300350.html.

14 "New Report Claims Ted Cruz Had Extramarital Affairs with FIVE Women—Including a Donald Trump Staffer! See How the Ladies Are Responding!" *PerezHilton*, March 25, 2016, http://perezhilton.com/2016-03-25-ted-cruz-sex-scandal-affairs-national-enquirer-report-katrina-pierson-donald-trump-campaign-spokeswoman/#.Wzu1BtJKiUl.

15 Leon H. Wolf, "Steve Deace Destroys Trump Surrogate Kayleigh MacEnany: 'Do You Have Any Integrity at All?'" *RedState*, April 28, 2016, https://www.redstate.com/leon_h_wolf/2016/04/28/steve-deace-destroys-trump-surrogate-kayleigh-macenany-integrity-video/.

16 Deace, "Has Trump Already Done More Than McCain or Romney Would Have?" *Conservative Review*, May 21, 2018, https://www.conservativereview.com/news/has-trump-already-done-more-than-mccain-or-romney-would-have/.

## Lie #3

1 Deace, "Jesse Jackson Was Right," *Townhall*, January 26, 2013, https://townhall.com/columnists/stevedeace/2013/01/26/jesse-jackson-was-right-n1495792.

2 Father Mark Hodges, "Jesse Jackson, Once Pro-Life, Runs Away from Question about Abortion as Black Genocide," *Life Site*, October 12, 2016, https://www.lifesitenews.com/news/jesse-jackson-once-pro-life-runs-away-from-question-about-abortion-as-black.

3 Steven Levingston, "John F. Kennedy, Martin Luther king Jr., and the Phone Call that Changed History," *TIME*, June 20, 2017, http://time.com/4817240/martin-luther-king-john-kennedy-phone-call/.

4 Brooks Jackson, "Blacks and the Democratic Party," FactCheck.org, April 18, 2008, https://www.factcheck.org/2008/04/blacks-and-the-democratic-party/.

5 Christian Red, "Jackie Robinson: 5 Famous Brooklynites Share Memories of Dodgers Legend on 70th Anniversary of Big-League Debut," *Daily News*, April 14, 2017, http://www.nydailynews.com/sports/baseball/jackie-robinson-5-brooklynites-recall-dodgers-legend-debut-article-1.3054912.

6 "Black Party Affiliation," Back Demographics, accessed July 3, 2018, http://blackdemographics.com/culture/black-politics/.

7 Oishimaya Sen Nag, "Largest Landslide Victories in US Presidential Election History," World Atlas, April 25, 2017, https://www.worldatlas.com/articles/largest-landslide-victories-in-us-presidential-election-history.html.

# ENDNOTES

8   "1973: Paris Peace Accords Signed," This Day in History: Jan 27, The History Channel, accessed July 3, 2018, https://www.history.com/this-day-in-history/paris-peace-accords-signed.

9   "Watergate Scandal," The History Channel, accessed July 3, 2018, https://www.history.com/topics/watergate.

10  Jonathan Hobratsch, "10 Worst Senate/House Defeats of the Last 100 Years," *HuffPost*, last modified January 5, 2015, https://www.huffingtonpost.com/jonathan-hobratsch/10-worst-senatehouse-defe_b_6106378.html.

11  YAFTV, "Ronald Reagan Addresses Young Americans for Freedom," Youtube video, 10:00, September 14, 2010, https://www.youtube.com/watch?v=RgfWieWrCvY.

12  Greg Forster, "Evangelicals and Politics: The Religious Right (Born 1979, Died 2000)," *The Public Discourse*, May 2, 2012, http://www.thepublicdiscourse.com/2012/05/5216/.

13  B. A. Robinson, "History of Catholic Presidential and Vice-Presidential Nominees in the U.S.," *Religious Tolerance*, last modified December 17, 2010, http://www.religioustolerance.org/rcc_poli1.htm.

14  Center for Applied Research in the Apostolate (CARA), *Presidential Vote of Catholics: Estimates from Various Sources* (Washington, D.C.: Georgetown University, 2016).

15  Lauren Feeney, "Timeline: The Religious Right and the Republican Platform," *Moyers*, August 31, 2012, https://billmoyers.com/content/timeline-the-religious-right-and-the-republican-platform/.

16  Ronald Reagan, *Abortion and the Conscience of the Nation*, rev. ed. (New Regency Pub, 2001).

17  Eric Metaxas, "Margaret Sanger Was an Outspoken Racist Who Hated Blacks, Campaign Tries to Polish her Image," *Life News*, August 3, 2015, http://www.lifenews.com/2015/08/03/margaret-sanger-was-an-outspoken-racist-who-hated-blacks-campaign-tries-to-polish-her-image/.

18  Ertelt, "Planned Parenthood Turns 99 Today: Has Killed 7 Million Babies in Abortions," *Life News*, October 16, 2015, http://www.lifenews.com/2015/10/16/planned-parenthood-turns-99-today-has-killed-7-million-babies-in-abortions/,

19  The Center for Medical Progress, "Investigative Footage," video, 10:17, July 26, 2017, http://www.centerformedicalprogress.org/cmp/investigative-footage/.

20  Deace, "The Biggest Liars in Modern American Political History," *Conservative Review*, July 31, 2017, https://www.conservativereview.com/news/the-biggest-liars-in-modern-american-political-history/.

21  Peter Hasson, "Broken Promise: Trump, GOP Congress Give Planned Parenthood $500 Million in Taxpayer Funds," *The Daily Caller*, March 23, 2018, http://dailycaller.com/2018/03/23/trump-gop-omnibus-planned-parenthood/.

22  Leah Jessen, "Tax-Funded Planned Parenthood Spending $38 Million to Push Hillary and Pro-Abortion Democrats," *Life News*, November 4, 2016, http://www.lifenews.com/2016/11/04/tax-funded-planned-parenthood-spending-38-million-to-push-hillary-and-pro-abortion-democrats/.

## Lie #4

1 CR Staff, "Big Baby 2.0: Uncovering the True Ties of National Right to Life," *Conservative Review*, October 2, 2015, https://www.conservativereview.com/news/big-baby-2-0-uncovering-true-ties-national-right-life/.

2 Philip Bump, "Donald Trump Will Be President Thanks to 80,000 People in Three States," *The Washington Post*, December 1, 2016, https://www.washingtonpost.com/news/the-fix/wp/2016/12/01/donald-trump-will-be-president-thanks-to-80000-people-in-three-states/?utm_term=.51b155c9c5fe.

3 Deace, Steve. "Jesse Jackson Was Right." Townhall. Accessed July 31, 2018. https://townhall.com/columnists/stevedeace/2013/01/26/jesse-jackson-was-right-n1495792.

4 Cabot Phillips, "VIDEO: Students Love Trump's Tax Plan...When Told It's Bernie's," video, *Campus Reform*, 3:30, October 20, 2017, https://www.campusreform.org/?ID=9997.

5 Pew Research Center, "A Deep Dive into Party Affiliation: Sharp Differences by Race, Gender, Generation, Education," *Pew Research Center U.S. Politics and Policy*, April 7, 2015, http://www.people-press.org/2015/04/07/a-deep-dive-into-party-affiliation/2/.

6 Michael Lipka, "How Many Jews Are There in the United States?" *Fact Tank*, October 2, 2013, http://www.pewresearch.org/fact-tank/2013/10/02/how-many-jews-are-there-in-the-united-states/.

7 Michael Gryboski, "Millennials Who Attended Evangelical Protestant Schools More Likely to Marry, Have Children: Study," *The Christian Post*, January 31, 2018, https://www.christianpost.com/news/millennials-who-attended-evangelical-protestant-schools-more-likely-marry-have-children-study-215814/.

8 Brad Plumer, "Why are 47 Million Americans on Food Stamps? It's the Recession—Mostly," *The Washington Post*, September 23, 2013, https://www.washingtonpost.com/news/wonk/wp/2013/09/23/why-are-47-million-americans-on-food-stamps-its-the-recession-mostly/?utm_term=.7a0178a45676.

9 Stephen Laboton, "Congress Backs Israel Embassy Switch, but Gives Clinton an Out," *The New York Times*, October 25, 1995, https://www.nytimes.com/1995/10/25/world/congress-backs-israel-embassy-switch-but-gives-clinton-an-out.html.

10 Veronica Stracqualursi, "John Kerry Engaging in Shadow Diplomacy to Salvage Iran Deal: The Boston Globe," *CNN Politics*, last modified May 7, 2018, https://www.cnn.com/2018/05/05/politics/john-kerry-iran-deal/index.html.

11 Matt Vespa, "Pelosi: Why Yes—Democrats Are Going to Raise Taxes if We Retake the House," *Townhall*, May 10, 2018, https://townhall.com/tipsheet/mattvespa/2018/05/10/pelosi-why-yesdemocrats-are-going-to-raise-taxes-if-we-retake-the-house-n2478607.

12 Paul Bedard, "Democrats Go All In for Gun Control as Top 2018 Issue," *Washington Examiner*, February 21, 2018, https://www.washingtonexaminer.com/democrats-go-all-in-for-gun-control-as-top-2018-issue.

13  Nate Cohn, "The Obama-Trump Voters Are Real. Here's What They Think," *The New York Times*, August 15, 2017, https://www.nytimes.com/2017/08/15/upshot/the-obama-trump-voters-are-real-heres-what-they-think.html.

## Lie #5

1  Deace (@SteveDeaceShow), "All we have to see, is that I don't belong to you. And you don't belong to me. Freedom," Twitter photo, May 4, 2016, https://twitter.com/SteveDeaceShow/status/727864167466569728.

2  Philip Klein, "Fred Upton's Cynical Reversal on Repealing Obamacare Show Why People Distrust Republicans," *Washington Examiner*, May 2, 2017, https://www.washingtonexaminer.com/fred-uptons-cynical-reversal-on-repealing-obamacare-shows-why-people-distrust-republicans/article/2621886.

3  Richard A. Viguerie, *Takeover: The 100-Year War for the Soul of the GOP and How Conservatives Can Finally Win It* (WND Books 2014).

4  Young Americans for Freedom, "The Sharon Statement," September 11, 1960, http://www.yaf.org/news/the-sharon-statement/.

5  Sandy Fitzgerald, "Ted Cruz Tries to Make Peace with Fellow Republicans," *Newsmax*, October 31, 2013, https://www.newsmax.com/Politics/cruz-peace-fellow-republicans/2013/10/31/id/534130/.

6  Sean Sullivan, "GOP Increasingly Fears Loss of House, Focuses on Saving Senate Majority," *The Washington Post*, April 9, 2018, https://www.washingtonpost.com/politics/gop-increasingly-fears-loss-of-house-focuses-on-saving-senate-majority/2018/04/08/6483ffc0-39bb-11e8-acd5-35eac230e514_story.html?noredirect=on&utm_term=.6c0de2d8fec7.

7  HuffPost, "Poll Chart: Nancy Pelosi Favorable Rating," last modified 2017, accessed July 3, 2018, https://elections.huffingtonpost.com/pollster/nancy-pelosi-favorable-rating.

8  Constitution Party, "Mission Statement," Principles, Constitution Party, accessed July 3, 2018, https://www.constitutionparty.com/principles/mission-statement/.

9  Libertarian Party, lp.org, accessed July 3, 2018, https://www.constitutionparty.com/principles/mission-statement/.

10  Linda Alchin, "Timeline U.S. Political Parties," Government-And-Constitution.org, 2015, accessed July 3, 2018, http://www.government-and-constitution.org/history-us-political-parties/timeline-us-political-parties.htm.

11  Richard Samuelson, "Jefferson, Adams, and the American Future," *Claremont Review of Books* 11, nos. 1 and 2 (Winter/Spring 2010/11), http://www.claremont.org/crb/article/jefferson-adams-and-the-american-future/.

12  Tre Goins-Phillips, "Faith-Based 'I Can Only Imagine' movie Stuns with Major Box Office Success: 'Hollywood Is Scratching Their Head,'" *IJR*, March 19, 2018, https://ijr.com/2018/03/1077292-i-can-only-imagine-movie/.

13  "GOP Caucus Results," 2012 Iowa Caucuses, last modified January 19, 2012, accessed July 3, 2018, http://caucuses.desmoinesregister.com/data/iowa-caucus/results/.

14  Fox News, "Bachmann Wins Iowa Straw Poll, Cements Her Top-Tier Status in GOP Race," *Fox News*, August 13, 2011, http://www.foxnews.com/politics/2011/08/13/finally-here-ames-straw-poll-first-test-2012.html.

15  Mike Allen, "Michele Bachmann Not Running Again," *Politico*, May 29, 2013, https://www.politico.com/story/2013/05/michele-bachmann-not-running-again-091972.

16  Dick Armey, "A Dobson's Choice for Conservatives?" *Fox News*, November 2, 2006, http://www.foxnews.com/story/2006/11/02/dobson-choice-for-conservatives.html.

17  Chris Pandolfo, "The Worthless, Fanboyish, Clickservative Culture of Pitiful Drama," *Conservative Review*, March 1, 2018, https://www.conservativereview.com/news/worthless-fanboyish-clickservative-culture-pitiful-drama/.

## Lie #6

1  LesGrossman News, "Ted Cruz Confronts Trump Supporters in Indiana FULL. 'Where's Your Goldman Sachs Jacket At,'" Youtube video, 8:45, May 2, 2016, https://www.youtube.com/watch?v=mvzcX4GQEHY.

2  *Idiocracy*, directed by Mike Judge, 2006 (Ternion).

3  Katie Pavlich (@KatiePavlich), "The fact that Republicans continue to fund Planned Parenthood with $500 million in taxpayer money is truly astounding," Tweet, March 22, 2018, https://twitter.com/KatiePavlich/status/976815567184252929.

4  Amy Mantravadi, "Luther's Life: A Curse Upon Erasmus!" *A Place for Truth*, accessed July 3, 2018, http://www.placefortruth.org/blog/luthers-life-curse-upon-erasmus.

5  Larry Getlen, "How McConnell and Chao Used Political Power to Make Their Family Rich," *New York Post*, March 17, 2018, https://nypost.com/2018/03/17/how-mcconnell-and-chao-used-political-power-to-make-their-family-rich/.

6  Joe Concha, "Erick Erickson: Ailes Took Me Off Fox News Because of McConnell Criticism," *The Hill*, March 19, 2018, http://thehill.com/homenews/media/379092-erick-erickson-fox-news-took-me-off-the-air-because-of-mcconnell-criticism.

7  "Kentucky," 270 To Win, accessed July 3, 2018, https://www.270towin.com/states/Kentucky.

8  "2014 Kentucky Senate Primaries Results," *Politico*, November 3, 2014, https://www.politico.com/2014-election/primary/results/map/senate/kentucky/#.WzvoOdJKiUk.

9  Jake, "Democrats Did Not Give Brat the Winning Edge over Cantor," *RedState*, June 13, 3014, https://www.redstate.com/ironchapman/2014/06/13/democrats-give-brat-winning-edge-cantor/.

## Lie #7

1  Ballotpedia, s.v. "Barry Loudermilk," last modified 2018, accessed July 3, 2018, https://ballotpedia.org/Barry_Loudermilk.
2  *Conservative Review*, "Rep. Barry Loudermilk Liberty Score," last modified July 3, 2018, https://pdfgenerator.conservativereview.com/pdf/412624. pdf#page=1.
3  Brendan Morrow, "Why Are the Members of the House Freedom Caucus?" *heavy.*, March 24, 2017, https://heavy.com/news/2017/03/who-are-the-members -of-house-freedom-caucus-list-of-representatives-do-not-support-health-care-bill-donald-trump/.
4  Joni Ernst. "2014, Joni Ernst - Squeal - Political Ad - Closed Captioned." The Closed Captioning Project LLC. YouTube. October 01, 2014. Accessed July 31, 2018. https://www.youtube.com/watch?v=zc8uLuHsNw0.
5  Conservative Review, "Sen. Joni Ernst Liberty Score," last modified July 3, 2018, https://pdfgenerator.conservativereview.com/pdf/412667.pdf#page=1.
6  Mattie Kahn, "Rand Paul's Hair: Let's Talk About It," *Elle*, May 28, 2015, https://www.elle.com/culture/career-politics/a28593/get-the-look-rand-paul-hair/.

## Lie #8

1  Dominic Patten, "'Pretty Little Liars' Series Finale Ratings Rise Over 2016, Dominates Social Media," *Deadline*, June 28, 2017, https://deadline.com/2017 /06/pretty-little-liars-series-finale-ratings-rise-freeform-1202121670/.
2  Julio Ricardo Varela, "The Latino Vote in Presidential Races: 1980-2012," *Latino USA*, October 29, 2015, http://latinousa.org/2015/10/29/the-latino-vote -in-presidential-races/.
3  Jens Manuel Krogstad and Mark Hugo Lopez, "Hillary Clinton Won Latino Vote but Fell Below 2012 Support for Obama," *Pew Research Center*, November 29, 2016, http://www.pewresearch.org/fact-tank/2016/11/29/ hillary-clinton-wins-latino-vote-but-falls-below-2012-support-for-obama/.

## Lie #10

1  Bruce Bartlett, "Medicare Part D: Republican Budget-Busting," *The New York Times*, November 19, 2013, https://economix.blogs.nytimes.com/2013/11/19/ medicare-part-d-republican-budget-busting/.

## Lie #11

1  Jeffrey M. Jones, "Americans' Identification as Independents Back Up in 2017," *Gallup*, January 8, 2018, https://news.gallup.com/poll/225056/ameri-cans-identification-independents-back-2017.aspx.

2  John Fund, "Bernie Sanders's Soviet Honeymoon," *National Review*, June 24, 2015, https://www.nationalreview.com/corner/bernie-sanderss-soviet -honeymoon-john-fund/.

3  Popular Technology.net, "The Coming Ice Age—1978," Youtube video, 1:32, March 1, 2013, https://www.youtube.com/watch?v=1kGB5MMIAVA.

4  Remy Melina, "Earth Day Co-Founder Killed, Composted Girlfriend," *NBC News*, April 21, 2011, http://www.nbcnews.com/id/42711922/ns/technology_ and_science-science/t/earth-day-co-founder-killed-composted-girlfriend/#. WzvtfNJKiUk.

5  Charlie Butts, "Kim Davis Tells Her Story," *One News Now*, April 16, 2018, https://onenewsnow.com/culture/2018/04/16/kim-davis-tells-her-story.

6  Gordon R. Friedman, "Appeals Court Upholds Fine Against Christian Bakers Who Refused to Make Same-Sex Wedding Cake," *The Oregonian*, last modified December 29, 2017, https://www.oregonlive.com/politics/index. ssf/2017/12/appeals_court_upholds_fine_aga.html.

7  Philip Bump, "Black Unemployment Hits a New Low—But Still Trails White Unemployment Significantly," *The Washington Post*, May 4, 2018, https:// www.washingtonpost.com/news/politics/wp/2018/05/04/black-unemploy-ment-hits-a-new-low-but-still-trails-white-unemployment-significantly/ ?noredirect=on&utm_term=.f20e23b299e9.

8  Ryan Saavedra, "WATCH: CNN's Brian Stelter Attacks Kanye West, He's 'A Gift to Racists,'" *The Daily Wire* video, May 2, 2018, https://www.dailywire.com /news/30162/watch-cnns-brian-stelter-attacks-kanye-west-hes-ryan-saavedra.

9  Jessica McKinney, "Ginuwine Refused to Kiss a Trans Woman on Live TV and Now the Internet Is at War," *Black Entertainment Television*, January 8, 2018, https://www.bet.com/music/2018/01/08/ginuwine-big-brother-celebri-ty-trans-woman-twitter-debate.html.

10  John Nolte, "Three DEMOCRAT-Run Cities Are Most Responsible for National Murder Rate Increase," *The Daily Wire*, April 18, 2017, https://www.dailywire. com/news/15489/three-democrat-run-cities-are-most-responsible-john-nolte.

11  Bump, "The Growing Myth of the 'Independent' Voter," *The Washington Post*, January 11, 2016, https://www.washingtonpost.com/news/the-fix/ wp/2016/01/11/independents-outnumber-democrats-and-republicans-but -theyre-not-very-independent/?utm_term=.47d494375a26.

12  Julie Zauzmer, "Holocaust Study: Two-Thirds of Millennials Don't Know What Auschwitz Is," *The Washington Post*, April 12, 2018, https:// www.washingtonpost.com/news/acts-of-faith/wp/2018/04/12/ two-thirds-of-millennials-dont-know-what-auschwitz-is-according-to-study-of-fading-holocaust-knowledge/?noredirect=on&utm_term=.34d68c66af95.

13  Paul Austin Murphy, "Antonio Gramsci: Take Over the Institutions!" *American Thinker*, April 26, 2014, https://www.americanthinker.com/arti-cles/2014/04/antonio_gramsci_take_over_the_institutions.html.

# ENDNOTES

## Lie #12

1 J.L. Bell, "5 Myths of Tarring and Feathering," *Journal of the American Revolution*, December 13, 2013, https://allthingsliberty.com/2013/12/5-myths-tarring-feathering/.

2 TheGreatWorker, "I'm Just a Bill (Schoolhouse Rock!)" Youtube video, 3:00, September 1, 2008, https://www.youtube.com/watch?v=tyeJ55o3El0.

3 SRCC07, "Sonia Sotomayor: Court of Appeals Is Where Policy Is Made," Youtube video, 0:28, July 10, 2009, https://www.youtube.com/watch?v=GdsK8ehTcMg.

4 "Natural Law and Sir William Blackstone," All About Philosophy, accessed July 5, 2018, https://www.allaboutphilosophy.org/natural-law-and-sir-william-blackstone-faq.htm.

5 Wbs, "Thomas Malthus (1766-1834)," UCMP Berkeley, accessed July 5, 2018, http://www.ucmp.berkeley.edu/history/malthus.html.

6 "Malthus, the False Prophet," *The Economist*, May 15, 2008, https://www.economist.com/finance-and-economics/2008/05/15/malthus-the-false-prophet.

7 Phil Moore, "What Your Biology Teacher Didn't Tell You About Charles Darwin," *The Gospel Coalition*, April 19, 2017, https://www.thegospelcoalition.org/article/what-your-biology-teacher-didnt-tell-you-about-charles-darwin/.

8 Kate Scanlon, "13 Things You Probably Don't Know About Planned Parenthood Founder Margaret Sanger," *The Daily Signal*, July 22, 2015, https://www.dailysignal.com/2015/07/22/13-things-you-probably-dont-know-about-planned-parenthood-founder-margaret-sanger/.

9 Becky Yeh, "7 Incredibly Shocking Quotes from Planned Parenthood Founder Margaret Sanger," *Life News*, February 23, 2015, http://www.lifenews.com/2015/02/23/7-shocking-quotes-from-planned-parenthood-founder-margaret-sanger/.

10 Ian Tuttle, "What Ben Carson Knows About Planned Parenthood," *National Review*, August 14, 2015, https://www.nationalreview.com/2015/08/planned-parenthood-ben-carson/.

11 Kevin Vance, "Sec. Clinton Stands By her Praise of Eugenicist Margaret Sanger," *The Weekly Standard*, April 15, 2009, https://www.weeklystandard.com/kevin-vance/sec-clinton-stands-by-her-praise-of-eugenicist-margaret-sanger.

12 Anders Hagstrom, "Movie About Man's Sexual Relationship with Underage Boy Selected as Best Picture by LA Critics," *The Daily Caller*, December 4, 2017, http://dailycaller.com/2017/12/04/movie-about-mans-sexual-relationship-with-underage-boy-selected-as-best-picture-by-la-critics/.

13 Samantha Allen, "Millennials Are the Gayest Generation," *The Daily Beast*, March 31, 2015, https://www.thedailybeast.com/millennials-are-the-gayest-generation.

14 Tenth Amendment, "Thomas Jefferson on Judicial Tyranny," Tenth Amendment Center, June 4, 2012, accessed July 5, 2018, https://tenthamendmentcenter.com/2012/06/04/thomas-jefferson-on-judicial-tyranny/.

15  A.G. Sulzberger, "Ouster of Iowa Judges Sends Signal to Bench," *The New York Times*, November 3, 2010, https://www.nytimes.com/2010/11/04/us/politics/04judges.html.

16  Robert Rouse, "Law, Liberty, and the Lord: Comparing the Bible to U.S. Laws," Soul Liberty, March 6, 2012, accessed July 5, 2018, http://soulliberty.com/law-bible/.

17  Lauren Carroll, "Ted Olson: Supreme Court Never Said Marriage Was Between a Man and a Woman in 15 Cases," *Politifact*, January 18, 2015, http://www.politifact.com/punditfact/statements/2015/jan/18/ted-olson/ted-olson-supreme-court-never-said-marriage-was-be/.

## Lie #13

1  John Adams to Massachusetts Militia, October 11, 1798, in *Founders Online*, https://founders.archives.gov/documents/Adams/99-02-02-3102.

2  American Chesterson Society, "Quotations of G. K. Chesterton," accessed July 5, 2018, https://www.chesterton.org/quotations-of-g-k-chesterton/.

3  jasonvuic, "What Do You Think of Your Team's Execution, Coach?" *Bucsnation*, September 19, 2016, https://www.bucsnation.com/2016/9/19/12972680/john-mckay-buccaneers-tampa-bay-quote-execution.

4  Sam Farmer, "Drew Pearson Recalls the First Hail Mary Pass," *The Los Angeles Times*, December 25, 2014, http://www.latimes.com/sports/nfl/la-sp-hail-mary-drew-pearson-20141226-story.html.

5  W. Cleon Skousen, *The 5000 Year Leap* (National Center for Constitutional Studies: 2007).

6  "Sign the Petition to Call for a Convention of States," Convention of States, accessed July 5, 2018, https://conventionofstates.com/.

7  Legal Insurrection, "William F Buckley Jr Harvard Faculty Quote," Youtube video, 0:35, December 16, 2015, https://www.youtube.com/watch?v=2nf_bu-kBr4.